Fin

The Finnish Spitz Dog Complete Owners Manual

Finnish Spitz dog book for care, feeding, grooming, health and training.

by

David Dunbarton

Published by: IMB Publishing

Table of Contents

Foreword

Are you an animal lover and looking to keep one as a pet? Then go for a Finnish Spitz dog! Why this particular type of dog? Well, let us tell you why: firstly, they are simply adorable and second, they can be your perfect pick-me-up-when-I-am-down pets for life. When it comes to toy dogs and sports dogs, you have over 25 different breeds. Now you must be thinking why there are so many breeds of toy dogs and what really sets each of them apart?

Well the answer is simple: their unique traits and characteristics. From their physical appearance to their behavior, every toy dog breed is different from the other. Some are playful, while others are really smart.

But this is the good thing about dogs. Unlike other pets, you can choose any dog breed to adopt and train them according to your needs and lifestyle. They can be your most loyal friend for life.

Dogs are known for their loyalty and intelligence. You can pick just about any breed- all they need is proper training and good care to enhance their positive behavior. They will behave as you train them- that's why they say "Your pet is your real shadow."

Adopting and training a sport dog is relatively easier than keeping any other dog breed simply because they are more manageable and only need a limited amount of space. But if you haven't kept a pet before, you might need a little training and this is where this eBook can help you.

Here in this eBook you will find everything you need to know about the Finnish Spitz breed – how to take care of it, how and what to feed it, how to go about its grooming and training concerns, and everything pertaining to this outclass breed.

Read through carefully before you decide to bring your canine companion home.

Chapter 1: Introduction

Have you ever wondered why dogs are called man's best friend? It is because they are extremely loyal and just like a sincere companion they will stand by you through thick and thin. They can make you laugh and make you forget all your worries when they cuddle with you. They are extremely intelligent and playful, which makes them more than just a pet. This is the reason that a dog keeper never feels lonely.

Each dog breed possesses different personality traits- some are hunters while others are working dogs. While there is a long list of dog breeds, it is easier to categorize dogs into various groups according to their personalities and habits. Dogs are classified into 7 main groups based on their personality traits. These are:

1. Sport dogs

2. Herding dogs

3. Toy dogs

4. Hound dogs

5. Working dogs

6. Non-sporting dogs

7. Terrier dogs

There are some dog breeds that possess mixed traits of two or more classes and the Spitz is one of these breeds. Breeds like the Spitz are currently included in the miscellaneous group because they possess mixed traits of sport and hunting dogs.

The dog breed discussed in this eBook is the Finnish Spitz, also known as the Finnish Barking Birddog and the Finnish hunting dog. These dogs were originally bred to hunt small birds and animals but they can easily be tamed and trained as domestic dogs. These are the "talkative" kind that will keep you busy and happy.

Being a medium-sized furry dog, it's really easy to keep a Finnish Spitz at home. Though they are originally hunters, with a little training and effort you can enhance their intelligence. They are extremely friendly and calm-natured dogs, and exhibit a very friendly behavior around children and other pets.

Being one of the favorite breeds of circus trainers, the Finnish Spitz has become the symbol of sport dogs. Spitz is a large family of northern dogs with pointed ears, thick fur and a curled tail. Famous dogs in this family include the Keeshond, Akita, Chow Chow, Pomeranian, Norwegian Elkhound and of course the Finnish Spitz.

The Finnish Spitz is probably the most famous dog in the Spitz family because of its friendly nature and intelligence. Compact in size and straight-legged, Finish Spitz, unlike other dogs in the Spitz family, are not heavy bodied dogs, and that's what set them apart from other Spitz dogs. You can easily train them according to your needs. Yes, you can't take the hunter away from Finnish Spitz, but you can always groom their other skills.

And that's where this manual can help you! Usually it is really easy to keep and train a Finnish Spitz because of their friendly nature, but if you haven't kept a dog before you need to learn a few things you need to be careful about while living with this dog breed. This eBook will give you an insight about everything that you need to know.

The Spitz family has a fox like appearance- they are usually recognized by fox eyes and a thick fur coat. The abundance of hair on its body further makes the breed look really fluffy and adorable. With the smiling expression on its face, it's impossible not fall in love with this breed. Of all Spitz dogs, the Finnish Spitz is the cutest. Due to a lot of fur, the dog might look bulky and heavy, but it's really light weight- and that's what makes them incredible jumpers.

Before you get influenced by the impulse of purchasing a Finnish Spitz and keeping it as a pet, it is important for you to know what a happy and healthy Finnish Spitz looks like and this eBook can help you learn every aspect about this breed. Plus, before you proceed and buy a Finnish Spitz for adoption, keep in mind that these dogs live up to a decade or more, and they need your special care and attention. So if you are up for such a big responsibility, then continue reading.

Whether you are a first-time dog owner or you have experience keeping pets, this eBook can help you train and keep a Finnish Spitz, but before proceeding any further ask yourself; do you really want a Finnish Spitz for adoption. Does this breed suit your needs? And if you can't decide, read this book. This manual contains everything you want to know about this breed. From their origin to medical concerns, you will find everything here. So go through the detailed information contained in this book about this breed and then decide if it's the right breed of dog for you.

And if you are worried about how, from where, and for how much should you buy a Finnish Spitz, then don't worry! This book is a complete manual about Finnish Spitz and contains answers to all your questions!

In addition to this, we have included detailed information about how to care for this breed, how to train it and how to make it people-friendly to adjust with your lifestyle.

So what are you waiting for? Start reading this book and learn all about Finnish Spitz.

Good Luck!

Chapter 2: Finnish Spitz- Small Dogs with Big Hearts

Don't get fooled by the innocent face and fluffy body of the Finnish Spitz- it's a hunter breed and it barks. This is probably the first thing you should known about this breed. The Finnish Spitz was originally bred for hunting and this is the reason it barks a lot. This breed is also called the talkative breed- because the Finnish Spitz makes different sounds for conveying messages to its owner. So if you want to keep a Finnish Spitz as a pet, get ready for a talkative and playful companion who will keep you busy all day. The breed is a really quick learner and you can easily train them. You have to give them a lot of time in the beginning to teach them and understand their language.

Being a hunter dog, the Finnish Spitz also makes an exceptional watchdog. So if you want to keep a dog for security concerns, the Finnish Spitz is just the right breed. It will keep your kids happy and protect you from intruders. Their excellent reflexes and intelligence sets them apart from other dogs of the Spitz family.

As a Spitz owner, you need to learn a few very important facts about this breed. You might find this breed hyperactive, but don't worry, it's in their blood. They are bird and small animal hunter dogs and that's why they are super active. So you need to keep a strict watch on them. They will need extensive physical and mental training- but here is the good thing about this breed, they are extremely intelligent and have an exceptional memory. Whatever you teach them, they will lock it in their memory for life. To keep this hunter and sport breed healthy and active, you will need to exercise it for around half an hour daily. Though the physical training depends on what you want to teach it, they are playful and like throw and fetch games. Oh and you will find Finnish Spitz very obedient.

The trickiest thing about keeping a dog as a pet is training them, but unlike other dogs, you will not have to put in a lot of effort in teaching the dog things from scratch. When it comes to intelligence, this breed is unbeatable. The Finnish Spitz responds positively to whatever you teach them. From basic training to sports, it's really easy to train this breed. You will learn training techniques in detain in later chapters.

As mentioned before, the Finnish Spitz has a lightweight body so you can train them as long as you want. But to keep the training sessions interesting, try to train your pet for 20-30 minutes every day. This will keep your pet active and extend its life. The Finnish Spitz has a furry body and they might shed hair during the winter- so if you have a fur allergy or asthma, reconsider your decision to buy a Finnish Spitz for yourself. Dogs love to cuddle and if you avoid them, they will become sad. If you can't be with them day and night, don't buy dogs.

As far as the grooming of a Finnish Spitz is concerned, it's really easy to groom these dogs. The Spitz is already a very gorgeous and attractive breed. All your pet needs from you is a little attention and care. The double coat of the Finnish Spitz is quite easy to maintain. Just brush the fur every week to keep it shiny and dust free. Daily brushing is also not good for dog's fur. It only increases fur shedding during the Fall. You will be learning grooming tips in detail in later chapters, but here it is important for you to know that Finnish Spitz have very sharp teeth and claws and if you don't trim their nails regularly, you might get hurt by them accidently.

Last but not least- if you want to keep your dog happy, let it live with you. Doghouses are a good idea, but keeping them tied in the backyard is just like punishing them. Just give them love and they will stay loyal to you for all their life. Breeds like the Finnish Spitz are extremely loving and friendly. They can be your most loyal companions for life; all they want from you in return is a little love and affection.

Chapter 3: Breed Specifications

The first thing you should know to get the right Finnish Spitz is breed specifications. These include their traits, adaptability, physical appearance and origin. Knowing breeding specs will also help you decide whether this breed fits your needs or not. So let's get started with the breed specifications of the Finnish Spitz:

1. Origin

This is probably one of the oldest breeds of dogs. The Spitz family has existed for centuries. The breed was originally developed for hunting small birds and animals but due to their extraordinary intelligence and friendly behavior, they were later discovered by circus trainers. This is probably the best trait of the Finnish Spitz- it can adjust itself in every environment. There are very few breeds of dogs that show such great adaptability and the Finnish Spitz is one of them.

The breed was developed in Finland by hunters for helping them in hunting small birds, but due to their distinct features and friendly attitude, the breed quickly gained popularity and now it's the national dog of Finland.

In the beginning of the 19th century, the citizens of Finland began experimenting with this breed. They started cross breeding Finnish Spitz with other dog breeds. The trend became so popular that by the mid-19th century, there were only a few original Finnish Spitz remaining in Finland. Realizing the gravity of the situation, two hunters took the initiative to save the original breed and ban the crossbreeding of Finnish Spitz.

To revive the original Finnish Spitz, the breed was transported to the United States. The breed soon became popular in the US and the government of the United States founded an official club for this breed in 1975 called the Finnish Spitz Club of America. It was then when the Finnish Spitz was recognized as a sports dog. Before being transported to the United States, the breed was only known as a hunter dog. The Finnish Spitz is one of the registered breeds of dogs by the AKC and it ranks 158th in the list.

2. Health and Grooming

Hunter dogs are physically active. They have strong immune systems and are less prone to viral diseases and infections unlike other breeds, but they naturally have the potential to develop genetic disorders. Just like humans, the Finnish Spitz also has the tendency to inherit genetic diseases from its parents. So to find a healthy puppy that is not at the risk of genetic diseases, you need to find an authentic breeder. Check the license of the breeder and only buy puppies from those breeders who give you a 100 percent guarantee about the health of the dog. To cross check breeder's claims, go to a vet and get the dog checked in detail. The vet will run several tests to examine the health of the puppy. You will learn more about how to pick a breeder in the following chapters.

Of all Spitz dogs, the Finnish Spitz is the healthiest and most active. They are usually less prone to degenerative diseases like diabetes, weak heart and other autoimmune conditions like epilepsy. But to be on the safe side, get the puppy checked by the vet before buying. It's really painful to see your pet in pain.

Only rely on the breeders that provide you complete documentation of the puppy's parents. There are certain health conditions which a vet might not detect in the beginning; this is the reason that it's really important for you to get assurance about the parents' health.

Buying a healthy puppy is not enough. After taking the puppy home, you are responsible for its health. Feed him well and take good care. It's true that the Finnish Spitz has a strong immune system that fights against infectious diseases, but it's up to you to keep them protected from all the viral diseases. Get them vaccinated. And yes, being a hunter dog, the Finnish Spitz needs to stay lightweight. So don't over feed them and make sure you give them a physical training session every day.

This handsome breed has a thick and soft double coat that makes them look very fluffy and irresistibly adorable. The upper coat is soft but the undercoat fur is thick and harsh-textured; this is because these are guard hair to protect the Finnish Spitz from extreme weather conditions. Though the Finish Spitz is not a messy breed, you will need to groom your pet to enhance its beauty. Here are some grooming tips for you to maintain the thick double coat of the Finnish Spitz:

Use a slicker brush (you can easily get from any pet accessories store) to brush the fur. It's effective for brushing off dust particles from the fur.

- Don't brush the fur frequently- once a weak is more than enough.

- Use a dog shampoo to clean the coat and minimize hair fall.

- Bathe your dog every month with the shampoo to keep the fur shiny and clean.

Other than fur maintenance, the rest is basic care. The Finnish Spitz is a very playful and friendly breed. They love to cuddle and that's why you should keep the nails trimmed. They are hunters after all and have sharp claws. Bad odor from ear indicates infection- so clean your dog's ears every week with a sot cotton ball. Get a good balanced-pH cleaner from a pet store and use it for cleaning ears. Oh, and dogs lick a lot. So brush your dog's teeth regularly to keep its mouth clean. Oral care is also vital for the overall health of pets.

The Finnish Spitz dogs are very quick learners. So familiarize your pup with the idea of cleaning and grooming right from the beginning. Again, this will be mentioned in more detail later.

3. Adaptability

Being the national dog of Finland, the Finnish Spitz has a very rich and interesting history. Their ancestors were especially adopted to accompany Finnish hunters and this is the reason they are so active. Again, although the breed was adapted for hunting small animals and birds, they can easily adjust any environment. They are infamous for being stubborn, but all they need is independence. They don't like being chained all the time. If you are adopting a Finnish Spitz then make sure you give them quality time.

The female Finnish Spitz is cool tempered but the male Finnish can become aggressive if they sense danger and this is the reason that the Finnish Spitz makes an exceptionally good watchdog. The Finnish Spitz is a very playful breed and they like the presence of children and other pets around them. However, they are not friendly with other canines they are not familiar with.

4. Special Needs

Although there are no special requirements of this breed, they need at least 2-3 hours of physical training daily. Being a hunter breed, the Finnish Spitz dogs are very active and playful. So you need to exercise them daily for 2 to 3 hours. Exercise includes physical training, running and playing. If you live in a rural area then make sure you don't let them off into farms as the Finnish Spitz an easily be mistaken as a wild fox. You can also take them with you on a morning walk or jog. The Finnish Spitz has a lot of stamina and they can run for hours without getting tired.

The Finnish Spitz dogs learn things quickly and it is really easy to train these dogs. But you need to be really patient while training these dogs. They might get aggressive and stubborn at times. Punishing them will only make them more stubborn. Motivate them with rewards and positive reinforcement and keep training sessions short and interesting. Another important thing you must keep in mind before getting a Finnish Spitz is that they have a very high-pitched voice and they bark a lot to express anger or communicate. So if you have an isolated backyard then that's good, otherwise you might need to install soundproof windows in your house so your neighborhood doesn't get disturbed.

The Finnish Spitz was originally bred in Finland and they are used to extremely cold weather. Although they are extremely adaptive, they might pant and sweat a lot during the summer. So you need feed them properly to maintain their energy levels. Lean protein and grains are really good for the Finnish Spitz, but make sure that the food you are giving to your dog is not overly processed. Preservatives and chemicals might cause indigestion and skin allergies in this breed.

And last but not least- the Finnish Spitz needs to be loved. They can be your best companions for life, but they only expect love and care from you in return. They don't like to be chained outside the house all the time. Allow them to sit, cuddle and play with you. This will keep them happy and healthy.

5. Finding the Right Breeder

Now that you are familiar with the basic traits of the Finnish Spitz and have decided to get one for yourself, you might be wondering where to start. The first step to finding the right dog is finding the right breeder. Getting acquainted to the breed and learning about its temperament, likes, dislikes and special needs might help you get prepared for dog adoption, but it is also really important to find a healthy dog and a good dog breeder can help you find the perfect pet. But finding the right breeder is not easy either- you need to be really careful and keep a lot of things in mind. Here in this section you will find all the information you need to spot an authentic breeder.

Traits of a Reputable Breeder

The easiest way to spot a good and reliable dog breeder is learning the traits of a reputable breeder. Here we have summed up some of the most important qualities of an authentic dog breeder who can help you find the perfect pet.

A reliable dog breeder always:

- Shows you all the dogs and allows you to visit the breeding club to ensure you that you have chosen the right place to get a dog.

- Keeps the breeding club clean and well maintained.

- Encourages puppies to play with you.

- Takes good care of breeding dogs and keeps them well fed.

- Knows all about the likes, dislikes, eating habits and other special needs of every breed.

- Keeps dogs in spacious kennels and allows them to play and exercise.

- Keeps only a few types of breeds to give all the dogs quality time and take proper care of them.

- Refers you to other reliable breeders if they don't keep the breed you are looking for.

- Takes care of the physical and mental need of dogs and allows them to socialize.

- Allows you to visit the puppy's parents so you can make sure that the puppy is not prone to any genetic disorders.

- Has contacts with vets and gets all the puppies checked regularly.

- Keeps a medical record of every breeding dog.

- Explains in detail the potential health risks and concerns of the breed you are looking for.

- Keeps the medical clarification certificate of the puppies' parents.

- Guides you about the measures that you must take before taking the puppy home.

- Offers you help with the initial training of the puppy.

- Sells the puppy after meeting the interested buyers in person and making sure that the person is capable of taking care of the puppy.

- Encourages to you keep visiting the puppy until you are satisfied. A good breeder will never force you to make the decision immediately.

- Allows you to get the puppy checked yourself before you take it home with you.

6. Questions to Ask the Breeder

The best way to judge if the breeder can be trusted or not is to ask questions. Here is a list of questions that you must ask when seeking a dog breeder:

For how long have you been breeding dogs?

This is probably the most important question that you must ask the dog breeder. Only choose the dog breeder with at least 5 years of dog breeding experience. This is because dog breeding is tricky, particularly if the breeder works with multiple breeds. Also ask for the certificate - don't trust the breeder blindly. A certificate ensures that the breeder can be trusted and he/she knows the technical stuff about dog breeding.

How many dog breeds have you worked with?

It is a common perception that a breeder who has worked with multiple dog breeds is better than the one who works only with selected breeds. Contrary to the general perception, you should trust only those breeders who focus on a few breeds (including the breed you are interested in). This is because breeders that work with multiple breeds don't give dogs quality time and a healthy breeding environment.

Ask the breeder if he/she has worked with the breed you want to adopt. If he/she says no, then ask if he/she has bred any similar breed. Dog breeds of the same class usually have similar eating habits, special needs and temperament. However, it is recommended to prefer a breeder who has worked with the breed you want.

Does the breed I am looking for have any congenital defects? If yes, what are you doing to work on these defects?

This is a trick question and the breeder's answer can tell if they can be trusted or not. Avoid any breeder who says that the breed you are looking for has no congenital defects, because that's not possible. Every breed is prone to congenital defects and there are some genetic problems present in every breed. You must do some research about the breed you are interested in before going to the breeder.

This way, you can crosscheck if the breeder is telling you the truth or not.

A good breeder, on the other hand, tells you all about the defects and potential genetic disorders the puppy is prone to. He/she will tell how you can deal with these disorders and possible ways to prevent the puppy from getting diseases. He/she will also guide you about the tests to find if there are any genetic defects in the puppy.

Do you keep the puppies' parents on site? Can I visit the puppy's parents?

If you really want a healthy dog, it is really important to see its parents. Almost every dog breed is prone to genetic disorders, so it is really important to make sure that the puppy you are about to adopt has healthy parents. Usually dog breeders don't keep both parents on site. Most breeders have mothers because they feed their pups. But if a breeder tells you that he/she has both parents- you should be a little conscious. This is because in most cases, breeders don't keep best matches for female dogs to avoid unplanned breeding. But if a breeder says he/she keeps both breeding parents, then it may mean that the breeding club is overly crowded.

However, you must insist on seeing both parents of the puppy. If the breeder has only one parent, ask the breeder about the other parent and pay a visit to make sure that the puppy is not prone to any incurable genetic disorder. If the breeder says he/she doesn't keep breeding parents, you must find another breeder.

You have all the right to visit the breeding site, but if the breeder does not allow you to interact with very young puppies, then it's okay. Very young puppies must be kept in a very healthy and isolated breeding environment. So if you are planning on adopting a puppy, make sure it's older than 4 weeks.

Can you brief me about the good and bad points of the puppy's parents? Are they healthy?

This is a tricky question and can help you judge if the breeder is genuine or not. It's true that the temper and qualities of every dog differ from the other. But every breed has some distinct traits that differentiate them from the other breed. For example, the Finish Spitz is a very playful and hyperactive breed. A good breeder is one who tells you about both the good and bad qualities of the breed. If the breeder starts enumerating all the amazing traits of the puppy, then he/she is just trying to impress you. No one is flawless. Every breed has some flaws and as a dog owner, you must know both the good and bad qualities of the puppy you are interested in.

Good breeders allow you to visit the puppy's parents and tell you about the salient features of the breed. They will you tell you about how the breed you are interested in is different from other breeds. It's true that every breed has its own characteristics but a good breeding environment and upbringing can improve the qualities of the breed. If the breeder is really genuine, they will tell you how he/she is trying to improve the breed and what you should do to train the dog.

Professional breeders have various titles like CD (Companion Dog), which is a benchmark for good training. If a breeder has dogs with such titles, it means you can trust them with puppy training.

Can you please tell me about the puppy's pedigree?

It is really important for you to gather information about the puppy's pedigree. Unprofessional and unauthentic breeders don't focus on facts about dogs' breeds. They are only interested in making money and selling their dogs. All they concentrate on is physical grooming. A good and trusted breeder, on the other hand, has sound knowledge about all breeds he/she works with. He or she will tell you all about the awards and titles the breed has been honored with. They will also tell you about the history and origin of the breed. To crosscheck the information provided by the breeder, you can also consult authentic online resources.

A good breeder is one who provides you information about at least 4 generations of pedigree. You can also ask about line of breeding and inbreeding.

Have you socialized the puppy? Where was the puppy born and raised?

It is really difficult to deal with puppies that are not used to interacting with other pets and people. Though friendliness and interaction skills of dogs vary from breed to breed, if trained properly, these skills can be improved to a significant extent. Ask the breeder if he or she has socialized the puppy from a young age or not. An ideal breeding environment is one where the puppies are raised together around daily household activities. This helps puppies get used to human's presence and noises around them.

In addition, a socialized puppy is easier to train and tame than a puppy that has been raised in an isolated environment. Visit the puppy you are interested in and spend some time with it. If it behaves normally around you and does not get intimidated by your presence, it means the puppy is well socialized. Examining the puppy's interaction skills is really important, particularly if you have kids or other pets at home.

Also ask the breeder if the puppy was born at the breeding club or not. This is important to know because puppies that are not born in a hygienic environment are more prone to common dog diseases. If the breeder says that the puppy was born in a garage or kennel, then ask if the puppy was immediately brought to the breeding club or not.

How many litters approximately does your breeding club have every year?

The annual litter production can tell you if their breeding facility is reliable or not. If the litter production of a breeding facility is more than 2 litters, it means that the breeding dogs are not provided a healthy and hygienic environment for breeding and puppies that are born and raised in such breeding clubs are usually prone to genetic defects.

Ask the breeder how many times a year he/she breeds the dogs. If the breeder says he/she only has puppies during particular months, it means he/she takes good care of the breeding dogs and provides the puppies with a healthy environment. So avoid any breeder who says he/she has puppies all year round.

If you ask a breeder if he/she provides a healthy breeding environment to puppies, they will definitely say yes. But asking about the annual litter production is an intelligent way to make sure the breeding club is reliable.

Can you give me any guarantees for this puppy?

No breeder can you give you a guarantee about a puppy's life or heath, but the least they can do is ensure you that the puppy has a sound medical record and its parents are healthy. And to make sure the breeder is not fooling you, get the puppy checked by a vet. However, there are some genetic disorders that can't be diagnosed, but if the breeding parents are healthy then the puppy is not prone to genetic diseases. So ask the breeder to show you the puppy's parents before finalizing your decision.

Also sign a contract with the breeder that they will take the puppy back if you are unable to keep it (for any reason).

Brief me on the adoption procedure and when can I officially adopt the puppy?

Adopting a puppy requires legal documentation and paper work and if you are adopting a dog for the first time you will need the breeder to brief you about the legal registration process. Usually breeders allow you to adopt puppies that are 8-12 weeks old. Plus the registration process will also take some time. A good breeder will help you complete all the legal documentation and registration process. This is the reason it is very important that the breeder you are choosing is certified.

7. What to Expect from the Breeder

Here is a quick list of the things that you expect from a reputable breeder:

- The breeder might ask you why you want a dog. Be honest while answering them, but make sure you are convincing.

- Depending on the breed you are looking for, the dog breeder might also ask about your family members. There are some dog breeds that are not friendly with kids and other pets (luckily, the Finnish Spitz is not one of them!).

- There are some landlords who don't allow tenants to keep pets, particularly dogs. Show the dog breeder a written agreement signed by your landlord that allows you to keep dogs and pets.

- Often dog breeders also require owners to sign a contract that you will return the puppy to the breeder if, for any reason, you are unable to take care of the puppy.

- Some dog breeders also visit the owners' house to make sure that the puppy will stay safe there.

8. Tips to Find the Right Breeder

A responsible breeder is one who cares more about the health and well being of the puppy than money. These days, finding a breeder is so easy that you can't really judge if the breeder is authentic and whether you can trust them or not. Puppies with unhealthy parents might suffer from a number of degenerative diseases and genetic disorders and it is really difficult to take care of a sick pet.

Such pets not only require special attention and care but you might also need to spend thousands of dollars on vet fees. So to avoid this hassle, it's better to pay a good breeder a few extra bucks than getting a sick puppy. Here are a few tips for you that can help you find the right breeder:

Set a Criteria

Make a checklist and make sure the dog breeder you are visiting meets the section criteria you have set. Dogs usually live for 10 to 20 years (depending on the breed), so you must be really careful while choosing the dog breeder. Your hasty decision or wrong choice will make both you and your pet suffer.

Your selection checklist should include the following:

- Must be experienced.

- Must have government approved dog breeding and training certificate.
- Must have good communication skills.
- Must have good knowledge about the dog breed you are looking for.
- Must keep a complete record about the breeding dogs and their parents.
- Must be professional and know all about puppy training.
- Must have a good reputation.
- Must keep dogs in a healthy and humane environment.

Referrals Are More Reliable

You can easily fall for scams and unreliable dog breeders if you only rely on the Internet as a source for finding a dog breeder for puppy adoption. A safer and easier way to find the right dog breeder is to ask for referrals. Go to some vets or ask your friends who know about a good dog breeder. You can also get reliable referrals from any local dog club. Never trust a dog breeder who sells puppies through a pet store. A reliable dog breeder is one who allows you to visit the breeding club, meet the puppy and its parents. This is the difference between an unreliable dog breeder and a professional one- a good dog breeder makes sure that your family setup and lifestyle meets the puppy's needs and you will provide a lifelong home to the pet, while local dog breeders only care about money.

Do Visit the Breeding Club for Yourself

Don't ask anyone (your friend or relative) to pick a puppy for you. Your satisfaction is really important. Pay a personal visit to the breeding club and select the puppy yourself. Learn all about puppy's medical history. Closely inspect the place where the puppy you are about to adopt was born and raised.

Chapter 4: General Appearance: Finding the Right Breed

If you want to adopt a Finnish Spitz, it is very important for you to learn about the physical appearance and other salient features of the breed to find the right puppy for you.

1. Salient Physical Features

The Finnish Spitz stands out due to its spectacular build and exceptionally fluffy double coat. They have a very athletic body and beautiful straight legs. The Finnish Spitz is known for its physical beauty- their sharp features, sharp muzzle and small round eyes make them irresistibly adorable. They have large triangular ears that give them an alert and active look. Due to their dark-colored fluffy coat and mouth shape, they closely resemble foxes.

Coat Colors

One of the signature features of the Finnish Spitz dogs that makes them different from other hunting breeds is their double coat. Usually every dog breed has a single layer of guard hair, which serves as sensors to sense danger and protect the dog from environmental factors. But what makes the Finnish Spitz different from other breeds is the additional layer of undercoat. The undercoat comprises of dense, fluffy fur with about 2 inches of long hair. The outer coat is meant to protect the dog so it consists of thick, harsh hair that can measure up to 2.5 inches long. The fur is significantly thicker and softer on the back of its thighs and neck than the rest of its body. The tail has long hair but it's very fluffy. Female Finnish Spitz dogs have a more refined and smoother coat than male dogs. You can easily pick a Female Finnish Spitz due to its fur quality and shine. The fur on the head and legs is shorter and easier to maintain. Despite the heavy fur and long hair, the Finnish Spitz can easily move its tail when it is excited or happy.

As a dog owner, you will have to take special care of the double coat. This is because the breed sheds undercoat hair twice a year. You will have to use the right hair product and brushing techniques to maintain and clean the thick double coat. If you have skin or respiratory tract allergies then trim the undercoat regularly and don't allow it to grow excessively. Though the dense undercoat makes the Finnish Spitz more cuddly and adorable, it's not good for you if you have health issues like asthma.

In order to make the fur appear more beautiful, a lot of dog owners allow the undercoat to grow excessively. But it's not easy to maintain and clean overly grown fur. Plus, it's also not good for the dog's health as they can develop different skin allergies. The Finnish Spitz is probably one of the most hairy dog breeds and as a dog owner you will also have to trim the hair under its feet.

As far as the coat color is concerned, the Finnish Spitz usually features dark-colored fur. They usually have black, brown and fawn hair. The coat color and texture might change with the dog's age, but a professional breeder can assess the coat color at the time of puppy's birth.

Height and Weight

The Finish Spitz has a unique and gorgeous square-shaped build, which means that the length of the entire body remains the same, just like a fox. Due to its stature and thick fur, the Finnish Spitz looks tall and heavy. To measure the exact length of the dog, breeders start measuring from the fore-chest or starting point of the shoulder to the rump. The only drawback of having a square-shaped build is a short back. However, female dogs usually have slightly longer backs than male dogs. Plus, female Finnish Spitz dogs are also slightly taller than male dogs.

The average height of male Finnish Spitz dog ranges between 17 to 20 inches, while female dogs average between 18 to 21 inches. However, the ideal height for male Finnish Spitz dogs is 18 inches and for female dogs is 19 inches. The weight of course varies with the physique, health and height of the dog, but it can range from 20 to 35 lbs. Despite the height difference, the male dogs weigh more than the female dogs and they have a broader frame.

2. Life Expectancy

Being a hunter breed, the Finnish Spitz is a very active breed. They exercise and run a lot and this is the reason that this is probably one of the healthiest dog breeds. But just like all other dog breeds, the

Finnish Spitz is also prone to some health concerns. If not taken care of and fed properly, the breed can develop slipping kneecap disorder and other neurological disorders like epilepsy. But these disorders are very rare and the Finnish Spitz is considered as a very healthy and active dog breed. The average lifespan of the Finish Spitz is estimated at about 10-15 years. But if fed and bred properly, they can also live up to 19 years or more.

3. Litter Size

The Finnish Spitz average litter size is around 4 to 7 small pups per litter. You must ask a professional breeder about the litter size of the breed to make sure you are getting the right dog.

4. Personality

The Finnish Spitz has a very lively and joyful personality. They are so friendly and loving that you just can't help falling in love with them. They get attached to their owner very quickly and show deep affection. The breed is definitely not overly affectionate but it craves love and interaction. They don't like being chained all the time and love to spend time with their owners. The Finnish Spitz dogs love to play and you will instantly catch the mischievous spark in their eyes when you look at them. They are not shy at all and have brilliant socializing and interaction skills.

If you have kids at your home and are concerned about the behavior of the Finnish Spitz around kids, then don't worry. The Finnish Spitz loves playing around children. The breed can be a little wary around new faces, but being a people-oriented breed, the Finnish Spitz does not take much time to gel in with new people. Being a very alert breed, the Finnish Spitz can also make very good and sensible watchdogs, as they are not aggressive and rarely attack people. They are super active dogs and love physical training and outdoor games. This is the reason they need very vigorous training to stay fit and happy. The Finnish Spitz is also friendly with other pets, but they might show aggression towards other pets if they feel threatened or insecure. Though the breed is generally very friendly and easy-going, its interaction skills also depend on the breeding environment. So make sure the pup was born and raised in an interactive and domestic environment.

5. Intelligence

The Finnish Spitz is an intelligent dog breed. These dogs are very playful and easy to train. These dogs were originally bred for hunting, so independence and enthusiasm is in their blood. You can train them for hours and they will not lose interest. But it is recommended to keep daily training sessions short and interesting. If you want to enhance their intelligence and other skills, reward them after every training session. They are very obedient and friendly and will never give you a hard time learning new things. However, repetitive training sessions can bore them. So, make sure each training session is different from the previous ones.

Chapter 5: Behavior and Habits

Every dog breed is characterized by its appearance, behavior and habits. It is true that training and the right breeding environment can enhance good qualities of dogs, but if you are planning on adopting a puppy, you should know all about its personality, behavior and habits.

Here, in this section, you will learn the general behavior and characteristics of the Finish Spitz that make them different from other dog breeds.

1. Is it Friendly?

The Finnish Spitz is a very friendly and interactive breed. Although the interaction skills and temperament also depends on the breeding environment in which it has been born and raised, the breed is naturally very cool-tempered. It's true that the Finnish Spitz was originally bred for hunting, but they are not at all bad-tempered. They love to play and interact with people. In fact, if you shut them outside the house all the time, they will become sad and quiet. So, if you are planning on getting a Finnish Spitz for yourself, keep in mind that you will have to give them a lot of time and attention. They are not overly cuddly like lap dogs, but they like the presence of people around them. Due to their friendly nature and playful attitude, they make perfect family dogs. The Finnish Spitz is naturally a people-oriented breed, but the breeding environment can significantly influence their interaction skills. If they are raised in a domestic environment with other pets, they will not get intimidated by the presence of children and other people around them. Plus, the Finnish Spitz is an easy breed to deal with and you can easily train them according to your needs.

2. Is the Breed Playful?

Despite being a hunter breed, the Finnish Spitz is not aggressive or stubborn. They are extremely playful and love outdoor games. But if you are thinking about adopting a Finnish Spitz dog, keep in mind that the dog needs a lot of exercise and physical training to stay fit and happy. Plus, they don't like repetitive training and need positive enforcement to learn new things. As a family dog, the Finish Spitz can play with you for hours. As long as you are loving towards it and take good care of it, it will never bore you.

3. Behavior around Other Pets

If you have other pets at home and are concerned about the behavior of a Finnish Spitz dog around other animals then don't worry. As a hunter dog, the breed is used to living in a wild environment with other animals, so the presence of other pets really doesn't bother the Finnish Spitz. Particularly, if a Finnish Spitz pup is born and raised with other pets, it will show very friendly behavior towards other pets. But in case you bring a new pet home, the Finnish Spitz might feel insecure and threatened by its presence. This is one thing about this breed- they are very possessive about their owners. They won't mind the presence of other pets, as long as you are paying good attention towards them. But if they feel your attention is divided, they might show an aggressive attitude towards other pets. They don't attack or fight with other pets, as long as they don't feel threatened by them. This is the reason the Finnish Spitz make exceptionally good watchdogs. Although the breed can be tamed easily, its skills in mingling with other pets and dog breeds also depends on the environment in which it has been raised. So make sure the breeder you are choosing for dog adoption keeps more than two breeds.

4. Behavior around Kids

If you are a first-time dog owner or are not familiar with the behavior and traits of the Finnish Spitz, you must be concerned about how the breed gets along with kids. Well, if you have kids at your home and are planning on adopting the Finnish Spitz, then this is probably the wisest choice you have made in dogs. The breed has a very playful nature and it loves the presence of children around it. If you are worried about the hunter instincts of the breed, then don't worry. The Finnish Spitz was bred to hunt small birds and animals, so they are not aggressive or wild. They are perfect for a family with kids. They are very active and love playing and children keep them busy. This is the reason that he breed is fond of kids.

5. Is It a Perfect Fit for a Loyal Pet?

Due to its friendly nature and good socializing skills, the Finnish Spitz makes a perfect family dog. Although it's true that you will have to take special care to puppy proof your house, the breed does not have any special needs other than training and affection. As a hunter dog, the Finnish Spitz needs regular exercise and vigorous training, but they make very loyal companions. Along with being playful and easygoing, the breed is also very obedient. They have a very good memory and will always follow the principles you have set for them.

So if you are looking for a perfect family dog, the Finnish Spitz is one of the best options, but here are some concerns you must keep in mind while adopting a Finnish Spitz dog:

The Finish Spitz dogs bark a lot. They have a high-pitched sound and make loud noises. So if you have a typical "peace loving" neighborhood, you might have to sound proof your house.

If you have a backyard and are thinking of chaining the pup in the backyard then it's certainly not a good idea. The Finnish Spitz does not like being chained in isolation. It likes to live as a part of the family and they might express their frustration by barking loudly if you don't let them live with you.

Chapter 6: A Sneak Peak at the Pros and Cons

As a dog owner, you must know about the strengths and weaknesses of the breed you want to adopt. The feeding, accommodation, health care and exercise of every breed are different. Learning about the traits of the breed you are looking for helps you prepare yourself for adoption. Dog adoption is not as easy as it may seem. It's not only the pup that adjusts to the family and new environment, but you will also have to make a lot of adjustments and learning about the key features of the breed can help you understand the needs and habits of your dog in a better way.

In this section, you will learn about the pros and cons of the Finnish Spitz.

1. The Best Features of Finnish Spitz

The Finnish Spitz is not only a hunter breed, but it can also make a prefect family dog as the breed is known for its friendly nature and loyalty. These dogs are not only irresistibly gorgeous, but they also have a number of other amazing features that make the Finnish Spitz a better breed for adoption than other dog breeds.

Here is a quick list at some of the many good features of the Finnish Spitz:

Temperament

This is probably the best feature of the Finnish Spitz dog- they are extremely cool-tempered and friendly and this is why they make the perfect family dog. They are wise, have an extremely good memory and are brave, active, inquisitive and faithful. Despite being a hunting dog, they are not at all aggressive. They love being around kids and other pets. However, they are very possessive about their owners and don't like it when their attention is divided. So, as long as you are giving quality time and affection to these dogs, they will behave very decently with other pets. It's true that the Finnish Spitz are very independent but you can easily train and tame them. When it comes to obedience, no other dog breed can beat the Finnish Spitz. You just need to give the Finnish Spitz love and care and it will stay loyal to you forever.

Energy Level

The Finnish Spitz is an extremely active and energetic dog breed and this is the reason you can easily train them. If you are a first-time dog owner and don't know anything about dog training, then you don't need to worry. The Finnish Spitz is the easiest breed to train because of their friendly nature and high energy levels. However, to keep them motivated, reward them after every training session. They prefer outdoor games and physical exercise. They are also good with following rules. Although the breed is slow in maturing, the Finnish Spitz dogs are not difficult to handle.

Perfect Family Dog

As mentioned before, they love spending time with family members. The Finnish Spitz dog makes for a perfect dog for large families with kids. They have excellent socializing skills. Although these skills can be enhanced if the breeder gives pups the right breeding environment, even if the dog was born and raised in an isolated environment, it can easily get adjusted with the idea of living among people. Adaptability and loyalty are the two best qualities of the Finnish Spitz. You can easily train them according to your family environment.

Trainability

Although the breed is pretty easy to train, the ease of training depends on the age of the puppy. It is usually easier to train small pups, mainly because they are small in size and more adaptable. They are very intelligent and learn new things at a quick pace. Plus, they are also very good at comprehending commands. They have a very good memory and rarely forget anything. The Finnish Spitz has an incredible stamina, and they don't get tired even after several hours of training. In fact, they need vigorous exercise to stay active and healthy.

Gait

The Finnish Spitz was bred for hunting. These dogs have a strong build and athletic legs. They have strong muscles and their gait is effortless. The breed can run very fast and this is the reason it can assist you in bird and animal hunting. Their gait can easily change from a slow walk to a gallop. The leg position is usually parallel when they are trotting. However, when running, their legs bend slightly. They have very strong bones and firm muscles. They can run several miles without getting tired.

The Finnish Spitz is the perfect pet for you, if you are looking for a dog that has the following traits:

- Has a medium-sized physique with lots of fur.
- Love to cuddle and spend time with the family.
- Has athletic body and loves playing games and physical; training.
- Adaptable and easy to train.
- Active, energetic and agile.
- Friendly and cool tempered with children and other pets.
- Have all the qualities of a good watchdog.
- Does not have a very short life span.
- Easy to feed.
- Less prone to genetic and degenerative diseases.

2. Things to Consider When Keeping Finnish Spitz as a Pet

Learning about the cons of the dog breed you want to own is equally as important as getting acquainted to its positive qualities. Here are some of the considerations that prospective Finnish Spitz owners must know:

Hair Shedding

There is no denying the fact that the double coat of the Finnish Spitz is their best physical feature, but the coat needs a lot of maintenance and care. The Finnish Spitz is a heavy shedder and if you have any kind of lung allergy, its excessive hair shedding can cause you serious health issues. However, there are a number of ways you can reduce the shedding to a significant extent. You can easily find fur care products and dog shampoos at any good pet store. Keep the double coat clean, dirt free and well brushed. But excessive brushing can also increase hair shedding.

Coat Grooming

If you are planning on getting a Finnish Spitz, then keep in mind that the breed needs a lot of grooming. It's true that the furry and heavy double coat makes the dog look very fluffy and adorable; you will have to take special care to keep the coat well maintained and clean. The Finnish Spitz is a super active breed- these dogs love freedom and playing outside. This is the reason their fur gets dirty quickly. Though the dog naturally has dark colored fur, if you don't keep it clean and dirt free, the fur will lose its shine and softness. Use a good dog shampoo to bathe your dog and brush the fur occasionally. You will need to trim the nails of your Finnish Spitz dog regularly because these dogs love to cuddle and play. They naturally have very sharp nails, so to avoid any accidental cuts, trim their nails every week. Also brush their teeth every day, as the breed is naturally prone to oral diseases.

Feeding

If you are a first time dog owner, you need to learn a lot about feeding dogs. Unlike other breeds, the Finnish Spitz does not have very complicated feeding requirements, but there are a few considerations you must keep in mind when feeding a Finnish Spitz dog. The daily-recommended amount for the Finnish Spitz is 1.5 to 2 cups of a good quality dog food. Feed the dog twice every day.

Although the meal size varies with the gender, age, physical routine and size of the dog, it is good to avoid over feeding the Finnish Spitz dog. Their stomach gets upset easily and they don't have a very fast metabolism. The appetite of the Finnish Spitz dogs also depends on how long and vigorous their training sessions are. The Finnish Spitz is not a very choosy breed when it comes to dog food. They will eat whatever you feed them. But make sure you give your dog good quality food. In addition, if the dog has some kind of allergy or genetic disorder, you must consult a vet before choosing a dog food for your pet.

The Finnish Spitz naturally has a very athletic body and strong muscles, but it's your responsibility to keep their beautiful body in shape. Feed the pet in calculated amounts. Don't feed it more than twice a day. Though malnutrition is bad for their health, obesity is more dangerous. It can reduce their stamina to exercise.

Here are some simple directions to examine the health of your dog at home. First have a glance at your pet; the waist must be visible. Then very gently place your palm on the back of the dog, and both thumbs on the back of its spinal cord in such a way that your fingers are spread in a downward direction. Now ever so gently run your thumbs through its spine. You should be able to feel the ribs- if you don't feel ribs, it means you need to reduce the meal size of your dog and increase its training time. On the other hand, if the ribs are visible, then your dog needs more food and less exercise.

Vocalism

A number of dog breeders don't inform about the barking habit of the Finnish Spitz, which might give dog owners a hard time later. So if you are planning on getting a Finnish Spitz, you might need to install soundproof windows in your house. The Finnish Spitz is very expressive and barks a lot to express its emotions and communicate. If you have kids at your house, the high-pitched voice of the Finnish Spitz might scare or disturb them.

Exercise Needs

Although there are no special accommodations or feeding needs of the Finnish Spitz, the breed needs plenty of exercise. They are extremely energetic and hyperactive and being a hunter breed, the Finnish Spitz needs physical training to stay healthy and in shape.

The breed is really easy to train, but for some dog owners, taking the dog on daily walks and giving it vigorous training might be tiring. However, if you chain the Finnish Spitz all the time and don't play with it, it might become aggressive and stubborn. One thing the Finnish Spitz hates about exercise is repetitiveness. You will need to put in some effort into keeping the training sessions interesting. Reward the dog with positive reinforcement and motivation. Play with the dog or simply leave it unchained in an open area. The

Finnish Spitz loves running. However, make sure you don't leave the dog on roads or streets. If you don't have a backyard, take the dog to a park. But keep a leash on it- the Finnish Spitz is a super excited dog and won't stay in one place.

Perspiration

The Finnish Spitz has a double coat and perspires a lot. Make sure you keep the dog well fed and hydrated. Keep the training session small and interesting. Give your Finnish Spitz a 45-minute slow walk daily to warm up the muscles. Don't take the dog outside during peak sunshine hours. Recommended hours for training are early morning and evening.

Keep the following considerations in mind before bringing a Finnish Spitz dog home:

- These dogs demand a lot of attention and quality time. If you want a pet, just for the sake of it, it's better to get some other pet than the Finnish Spitz.
- The Finnish Spitz is hyperactive and needs a lot of exercise daily. Without physical training and exercise, they can become aggressive, glum and easily irritated.
- You can't chain them in your backyard all the time. The Finnish Spitz can suffer from "isolation anxiety" when left alone.
- When not fed or attended to properly, the Finnish Spitz can become really stubborn and tough to handle.
- They are emotionally sensitive to depression and stress.
- The breed is a heavy shedder and not recommended for asthma patients.
- The Finnish Spitz is a very vocal breed. It has a high-pitched voice and barks a lot to express different emotions.

3. Information about Acquisition
Now that you are familiar with the positive and negative sides of the Finish Spitz, it's time to move on to the next step- that is the acquisition process. If you have decided that the Finnish Spitz is the right breed for you, this section will particularly come in handy!

We have already discussed the importance of finding the right breeder in previous chapters, but what you need to know now is the options of pet adoption that you have. You have three options of getting a puppy:

- You can adopt a Finnish Spitz puppy from any dog rescue group.
- You can go to a reliable pet store.
- You can opt for a dog adoption club.

Regardless of what option you choose, you will have to go through a registration process to legalize the adoption. This section deals with the pros, cons and considerations of different ways of dog adoption and what you need to do to get your puppy registered from AKC.

4. Adopting a Puppy from A Rescue Group

Animal rescue groups are not like animal shelters or clubs. Unlike adoption clubs that have a central location, where various types of dog breeds are kept together, a dog rescue system provides a temporary foster home to stray puppies. Usually these groups are run by animal lovers who work in a closed network and take care of small puppies and stray dogs. Dogs in rescue groups are kept for a particular evaluation period, in which they are given basic healthcare and training.

For disabled puppies, rescue groups provide a permanent shelter, but puppies that are healthy and ready for adoption are put on sale. Getting a puppy from a rescue group seems like a feasible and simple option, but it has its own pros and cons. Let's have a look!

a. **Pros**
- A rescued dog is usually trained in a domestic environment. It is used to human voices and the presence of people around it. Plus the foster family spends a good deal of time with the dog and can tell you about the habits, traits and special needs of the dog in a better way. Rescue groups keep multiple dog breeds together sometimes, which makes rescued dogs really tolerant, patient and adaptable.
- The foster family can also brief you on training the dog. Usually the toughest period of pet adoption is the basic

training, but rescue dogs receive their initial training at foster houses- so they are comparatively easy to train.

- Rescue groups also give basic health protection to dogs before selling them. For example, you don't need to worry about the initial vaccination and genetic health problems. However, you always have the option to seek to make sure that the puppy is healthy, before adopting it.
- Rescue dogs are quicker at learning commands compared to pampered dogs that are born and raised in a club.

b. Cons

- For obvious reasons, you can't rely on the information provided by rescue groups. Authentic shelters or clubs keep a complete health record of the puppy as well as its parents. Rescue dogs usually come from an unknown background, and they might have genetic problems. Plus, there are some degenerative diseases that are not dominant from the beginning and even a vet can't tell you if the puppy you are buying is prone to these diseases or not. The only way to find it is to check the health record of a puppy's parents, which rescue groups usually don't have.
- Rescue dogs are not as easy to tame as shelter dogs. They usually have behavioral and socialization issues.
- Usually, you can't get a very young puppy from a rescue group. You will usually find middle-aged or adult dogs, but it is not easy to find a puppy at rescue center. However, the best age to train and adopt a dog is when it is young.
- Rescue groups keep common stray dog breeds. And if you are looking for a breed like the Finnish Spitz, which is an uncommon breed, rescue groups might not be able to help you.
- As far as the price is concerned, buying a dog from dog club is cheaper than from a rescue group. However, you will have to invest in vaccination, basic health care and flea prevention if you get a puppy from a shelter house. Rescue groups provide basic facilities to dogs at foster homes.
- Another disadvantage of getting a puppy from a rescue group is they are usually not registered. So you will have to complete the registration process on your own. A registered

club or pet store usually hands over you the puppy after completing all the legal procedures.

- Recue group owners are not professionals. They are usually dedicated animal rescue workers, who work for animal rights. So they might not provide you accurate information about the dog breed you are looking for.

5. Adopting a Puppy from a Pet Store

The next place you can go to find a Finnish Spitz for adoption is a pet store. If you are a person with no knowledge about dog breeds, it is better for you to opt for a good pet store in town than go to a random rescue group. But it is really important for you to choose a good and reliable pet store, because every pet shop claims that they have the best dog breeds, which is not always true. It's true that you can easily find lots of puppies in a pet store, and they might belong to a good breed, but if a pet shop owner says that the puppies in the shop have come from a local breeder then he/she is not telling you the truth. This is because no responsible breeder sells its trained and well-fed puppies to pet stores. Puppies that are bred in clubs are usually raised in a very lavish environment. On the other hand, pets in local shops are usually kept in cramped cages with a lot of other pets. This increases the risk of contagious diseases and impacts the overall health of puppies. So a responsible breeder would never give his/her puppies to a pet shop.

However, there are authentic pet shops that keep original and rare dog breeds and keep them in a very good environment. If you are opting for a pet shop for dog adoption then make sure that the shop is not overly crowded and the storeowner knows a good deal about the breed you are looking for. To make sure that the shop owner is giving you the right information about the dog, do some research on the breed before going for adoption.

Another thing you must keep in mind to avoid scams when adopting dogs from a pet store is never choose a pet shop that says they keep dogs from USDA (United States Department of Agriculture)-certified breeders. This is because USDA is a department that only deals with farming and has nothing to do with dog breeds. The department only focuses on aspects like the legal documents of the breeder and breeding environment of the shop where the pets are bred. As long as all the documents are in order and the breeding environment is healthy, USDA will pass the pet shop. It is not concerned about the knowledge of the breeder or his/her experience. So if a pet shop owner says that he or she has USDA-certified breeder's dogs, it means that here will be no completing legal paperwork for dog adoption. But it does not guarantee that the breed is original or the breeder is reliable.

When going to a pet shop for getting a puppy, you must keep in mind that the puppy's health is not guaranteed. If any pet shop owner says that the puppy's health is guaranteed then don't trust them. This is because unlike certified breeders, pet shop owners don't keep the health records of puppies' parents. Dogs are naturally prone to genetic diseases, so to make sure you are getting a healthy puppy it is important to know about the health of its parents. Another reason you should not trust pet shops when it comes to health is that they keep pets in a very crowded environment and small puppies can easily contract diseases from other pets. Plus, it also impacts their personality and socialization skills.

1) **Pros**
   - A dog born and raised in a pet shop with other pets is usually trained in a domestic environment. It is used to living with other pets and is familiar with human voices.
   - If the pet shop is good and the pet shop owner is experienced, he or she might know a good deal about training dogs and their habits (even if not certified). He/she can tell you about habits, traits and special needs of the dog in a better way.
   - Pet shops often keep multiple dog breeds together sometimes, which makes rescued dogs really tolerant, patient and adaptable.
   - The toughest period of pet training is the initial days, but dogs raised as pets receive their initial training in a very domestic environment with other pets. So they are comparatively easy to train.
   - Good and reliable pet shops give basic health protection to dogs before selling them. In that case, you don't need to take your dog for the initial vaccination after adoption. To make sure that the pet is vaccinated, you can seek to make sure that the puppy is healthy before adopting it.

- Dogs raised with other pets are quicker at learning commands compared to pampered dogs that are born and raised in a club.

2) **Cons**
    - Not all pet owners get puppies from reliable and registered breeders (mainly because licensed puppies are expensive) so you can't rely on the information provided by pet shop owners.
    - Usually pet shop owners don't have the complete health record of the puppy as well as its parents. Puppies at local pet stores come from rescue groups or local breeders and they have very little knowledge about their background and genetic history. You can go to a vet to get the puppy tested but there are some degenerative diseases, that are not dominant from the beginning and even a vet can't tell you if the puppy you are buying is prone to these diseases or not.
    - Dogs at pet shops are usually born and raised with a lot of other dogs with different qualities and backgrounds. This is the reason that pet store dogs are not as easy to tame as shelter dogs. There are chances of behavioral and socialization issues in these dogs.
    - Pet stores usually don't keep very young puppies. They have groomed and adult dogs and these dogs are not very adaptable. Plus, you will also find it difficult to teach new things to an adult dog because the best age to train and adopt a dog is when it is young.
    - If you are looking for the original breed of the Finnish Spitz, then the pet store is not a good place to go. You might find a puppy at a cheaper price in pet stores but they keep all kinds of breed. A breed like the Finnish Spitz is uncommon and you cannot find it in local pet stores.
    - The most important concern for most pet owners when getting a puppy is price. Local breeders usually sell puppies to pet stores, where they are groomed for adoption. You will not find quality breeds at pet stores and this is the reason that you can find puppies at a relatively cheaper price at pet stores than licensed breeders.

- Another con of adopting a Finnish Spitz puppy from a pet store is that they are usually not registered. So you will have to bear all the registration expenses and complete the process on your own. A registered club, on the other hand, usually hands you the puppy after completing all the legal procedures.
- Many pet owners don't consider this fact while getting a puppy from a pet store but this can save them from a lot of problems. Pet store owners are not professionals. They just have good connections in the pet market and they buy puppies from breeders. So they might not provide you with accurate information about the dog breed you are looking for.

6. Adopting a Puppy from a Dog Club

Another option you have to get a puppy is go to a good breeder. You can find a number of dog clubs online who are registered with organizations like AKC and that sell licensed dogs. You can trust these clubs with the quality of the breed. Dog clubs also keep heath records of the puppy's parents to ensure pet owners that the puppy they are buying is healthy and does not have any genetic disorder.

Is Registration Important?

If you are a first-time pet owner, keep one thing in mind- getting your pet registered is a must. This is because a registration license gives you important information about the pet's background and tells you the date on which the puppy was born. However, many pet owners confuse a registration certificate with health certificate. A registration certificate is only a legal document that tells you complete information about the puppy's parents and its age, but it does not guarantee the health of the puppy. Whether the puppy is registered from the AKC (American Kennel Club) or the Kennel Club, the registration certificate cannot tell anything about the quality of the breed. The certificate does not even tell anything about the puberty of the puppy.

But it is very important for you to determine the background of the puppy you are adopting. Of all pets, puppies are the most prone to degenerative and viral diseases. So it is really important for pet owners to get complete information about puppy's parents and make

41

sure that the puppy is not at risk of any disease. When a dog is registered, the registration institute gives it a call name and a legal name. Breeders usually keep the registered name because it easily allows them to track the puppy's record, but as a dog owner, you have the liberty to choose the call name.

If the puppy is a purebred, the registration certificate can also help you track the entire family tree of the puppy. You can also learn about special traits and basic information about the dog by getting information about the puppy's pedigree. To make sure that the breeder you are choosing is authentic or not, ask him/her about the pedigree of the dog. Authentic breeders know all about the bloodline of the puppy and they can tell you about the honors and tilts the breed has been awarded.

However, if you want to know about the health of the puppy, get it checked by a good vet. Although genetic disorders can't be diagnosed at an early stage, a vet can ensure that the puppy does not have any behavioral problems or viral ailments.

7. Estimated Price of Breed

If you are planning on getting a puppy, keep in mind that it's just not a one-time expense- there are a number of ongoing expenses associated with owning a puppy. Although the basic price of the Finnish Spitz depends on the seller or dogs' club, you can have an idea about the average price of the Finnish Spitz from online websites (but make sure your resources are authentic). Most pet stores and clubs have online stores where the prices are mentioned. The average price of the Finnish Spitz can cost you somewhere between $1,000-$2,000, depending on the age, gender, and health of the dog. A vaccinated and registered Finnish Spitz will obviously cost you more than an unregistered puppy. If you are looking for a Finnish Spitz in the US, the most authentic place to learn about dog prices is AKC (American Kennel Club) and for the UK residents, it's The Kennel Club.

Besides the basic price, other expenses that you must keep in mind before getting a puppy include:

- Dogs at local pet stores and shelters are usually not vaccinated. Early vaccination is very important to protect puppies from diseases like rabies. However, breeders usually administer basic vaccines and immunity boosters. One time vaccination is not enough. You will have to get your Finish Spitz checked regularly to protect it from common ailments.
- Another expense that's included in the basic price of the dog is registration fees. If you are getting the dog from a breeder, you don't have to worry about registration because registered breeders sell licensed dogs. But registered dogs are usually more expensive than shelter dogs. However, the registration costs depend on the state you are living in. Every country has its own registration process and fees structure, but usually the registration cost ranges between 8 to $15.
- Other miscellaneous expenses include food and shelter. You will have to upgrade the kennel size as the puppy grows. The Finish Spitz does not like congested doghouses. As far as the food is concerned, the Finnish Spitz is a really easy breed to deal with and it does not have any special needs.
- You will also have to install soundproof glass as the Finnish Spitz has a very high-pitched voice and barks a lot; this can bother your neighborhood.
- If you are shipping the dog from some other country or city, you will have to pay shipping charges.

8. How Can You Reduce Expenses?

There are some expenses that you can't avoid, like accommodation, food and basic healthcare, but you can definitely reduce them if you take care of a few things:

- Take the puppy to the vet before making the final payment and make sure it does not have any disease and is vaccinated.
- Ask the breeder to give you the medical record of the puppy. This is important because usually genetic disorders are nit diagnosed at early age.
- Also make sure that the puppy you are buying does not have any behavioral issues.

- Try to negotiate with the breeder for concession and go to multiple pet owners to get the best deal in terms of price and breed quality.

9. Guidelines for Finding Finnish Spitz in the US

Although there are a number of places you can get a Finnish Spitz for adoption, for the original breed you need to go to the best places around. If you are looking for the original Finnish Spitz in the United States for adoption, then there is no better place than the American Kennel Club. The club is the biggest club in the US that offers registration to a wide range of dog breeds and the Finnish Spitz is one of those breeds.

While there are a number of ways for dog adoption, it is very important for you to make sure that the breeder is authentic. For that, you just need to ask the breeder to show the registration papers. Usually breeders claim that the breed you want is pedigree, but only a registration certificate approved by a recognized organization can validate their claims. The American Kennel Club, being the biggest and the oldest dog registration club in the United States, offers registrations for purebred dogs only. Unlike other dog agencies that register dogs without inspecting the breeder about its parents and pedigree, the AKC makes sure that the breed is original. Its standards are strict and even the slightest deviation from eligibility criteria can disqualify the dog.

The AKC is the only club that requires the breeder to provide complete information about the lineage of the puppy for issuing a registration certificate. It does not offer registration for random puppies with no background even if they are born and raised by an authentic breeder. For registration, the breeder must provide a health record of the puppy's parents, other relatives and also grandparents (if possible). The AKC has high standards and only the best fit the eligibility criteria. This is the reason that AKC certification is so reliable and has so much value.

The AKC certification not only validates the authenticity of the breeder and dog breed, but the organization can help you find a good breeder where you can find original and rare dog breeds like the Finnish Spitz. There is a forum on the official website of the AKC where you can find a list of breeders who sell certified dogs. You can also look for breeders in your state with respect to the breed you want to adopt. This can certainly make it easier for dog owners to find reliable breeders in their state who can help them find the dog of their dreams.

Another way to find a Finnish Spitz for adoption is online shopping- but it is not a safe deal, especially if you are a first-time dog owner. You can easily fall for scams and frauds, which is a common issue in online shopping. Until and unless someone refers you to any online pet store, avoid opting for this option. And if you chose a dog online, make sure you meet the dog and the breeder before making the payment. If you have read the previous section about physical features and special qualities of the Finnish Spitz, you can easily spot an original Finnish Spitz.

If the breeder is located in a distant region, you might find it cumbersome to make a long trip, but it is crucial for finding the right dog. Try not to settle for phone calls- a breeder can easily fool you on the phone. Don't believe anything the breeder tells you about the dog unless you have visited the dog.

Never settle for phone calls when it comes to breeders' references. It might be cumbersome to make the trip to a distant region but it usually pays off well in the end. Conducting fraud in phone calls is also quite possible. Don't believe anything until you've seen it with your own eyes and heard it for yourself!

Another option to buy a Finnish Spitz in the United States is to get it shipped. Although choosing the Finnish Spitz online and getting it shipped might sound easy and hassle free, just like online shopping, shipping is also risky. Even if the breeder is reliable and the puppy is an original breed, it is very important for you to meet the puppy several times before you bring it home. Make sure that the puppy has no behavioral issues and can easily adjust to your family.

If you are getting the puppy registered yourself then you have to bear all the expenses yourself. But if you are getting the puppy from an AKC registered breeder, then you will get a certified puppy. Registered puppies are slightly more expensive than random puppies, but a registration certificate tells you all about the parents of the puppy that can help you track the origin of the puppy. You can also find the health record of the puppy's parents and make sure that the puppy you are buying belongs to a healthy background and is not prone to any genetic disorders.

10. Guidelines for Finding Finnish Spitz in the UK

Just like the American Kennel Club is considered as the most reliable and authentic registration organization, every state has its own registration standards and authorities. If you are living in the United Kingdom, then AKC registration papers might not work. The authority that is considered equivalent to the AKC in the United Kingdom is the Kennel Club.

The Kennel Club (like the AKC) is the most reliable and oldest registration club in the UK. It also offers registration for a wide range of dog breeds including the Finnish Spitz. The official website of the Kennel Club provides you with general information about the Finnish Spitz like its origin and indicators that can help you spot the original breed. Registration standards of the KC are also quite strict, but unlike the AKC, it also certifies mixed and crossbreeds, provided the breeder has complete information about both patents of the puppy. If both parents belong to original breeds, then only a puppy can qualify for certification. The Kennel Club also offers information about reliable breeders in the UK that sell original breeds and have compete information and health records of the puppy's parents.

Just like in the United States, you also have plenty of options to buy the Finnish Spitz in the UK, but a KC certificate validates that the puppy belongs to the original breed. Plus, with complete information about the puppy's parents you can make sure that the puppy is healthy and does not have any health problems. Preferring a certified dog over a random dog is probably the best way to discourage unhealthy and unprofessional breeding habits. The Kennel Club has the list of all the professional breeders that follow the ethical code of breeding puppies. So instead of counting on referrals and online resources, simply visit the official website of the Kennel Club and go to the right breeder in the first attempt.

Even if you are opting for online breeders or local stores, visit the breeder and the puppy multiple times. Evaluate the breeding environment and make sure that the breeder follows standard guidelines of healthy breeding. However, authentic breeders don't sell puppies online. They meet the owners to make sure that they can take care of the puppy. It is better to evaluate the breeder and the puppy before making the final transaction because once transferred, the transaction can't be reversed that easily.

11. How to Identify the Original Breed

Although the physical features and other important traits of the Finnish Spitz have already been discussed in previous chapter and the information is more than enough for you to identify an original Finnish Spitz, there some health concerns that you must keep in mind while looking for a Finnish Spitz. Every dog breed has a potential to develop some kind of disease. The Finnish Spitz is a tough and strong breed, but it is prone to hereditary diseases. Most of these health issues are incurable, and the only way to save yourself from the hassle of raising a sick puppy is to check the medical record of the puppy's parents. If the puppy has a healthy lineage, get it otherwise look for another puppy. You can take the puppy to a vet for general screening, but there is no test that can detect probable genetic health risks in a dog. Common disorders in the Finnish Spitz include CHD (Canine Hip Dysplasia).

If the puppy is genetically healthy, you can take measures to improve its immune and overall health (that you will learn later in the book.) So, the best way to get an original and healthy Finish Spitz is go to a registered kennel club in your state and ask them for referrals. Certified breeders only raise original and genetically healthy puppies- so you don't have to worry about finding the health record of the puppy and its parents.

Before you get to the purchase stage, there are a few general signs of good health to be aware of when choosing a healthy puppy from a litter. You will learn about common health issues in the Finnish Spitz and ways to cope with these issues later, but here are some indicators that can help you identify a healthy and active Finnish Spitz. Have a look:

Health

Usually dog owners like chubby dogs they can cuddle with, but make sure that the puppy is not fat. Obesity in the Finnish Spitz can lead to severe health issues. Similarly, the puppy should not be malnutrition.

Breathing

Make sure you meet the puppy several times before you make the final decision. Inspect it closely and let it run in the open field. A healthy puppy will not pant; it will breath calmly. Plus, also make sure that there are no signs of coughing or sneezing. Puppies can quickly contract viral diseases like the flu when they are raised with other pets.

Coat

The Finnish Spitz has a heavy coat and it sheds heavily, but make sure that the fur is well maintained. Make sure there are no fleas or bald spots. The Finnish Spitz has a double-layered coat that is very difficult to maintain.

Vision

Being a hunter breed, the Finnish Spitz has a very sharp vision. To make sure the puppy does not have any sight issues, there is a simple test. Throw a piece of wood to the puppy and let it fetch it. If the puppy fetches the wood successfully, it means it has perfect eyesight. Plus, also check the puppy's eyes physically. Make sure the puppy has clear and bright eyeballs without any discharge.

Hearing

The Finnish Spitz is a very friendly breed and likes to socialize. It will instantly respond if you call it. However, if it does not respond, it might have some problem with its hearing.

Activeness

The Finnish Spitz is usually a very active and energetic breed and loves running and playing. If the puppy looks dull and lazy, then it might have some health issue. Get it checked by a good vet before getting it.

Gait

Being a lightweight dog, the Finnish Spitz can jump easily. Let the dog run and jump, and if you notice any problem in its walking, reconsider your decision. The breed, being a superlative hunter breed, needs a lot of physical training and exercise to stay healthy. A less active physical routine might impact the overall health of a Finnish Spitz dog.

Genitals

It is very important for you to make sure that the puppy has no genital issues. Look for any type of viscous discharge in or around their genital regions.

12. Registration

Registration authorities are different in every state, but registration requirements and standards are more or less the same. For getting your puppy registered, dog owners have to fill the application form jointly with the breeder. As the current owner of the dog, breeders have to fill out most of the form. Usually the registration application in every country requires the following information to be provided:

- Accurate age of the puppy (along with the date of birth)
- Sex of the puppy
- Original coat color and birth marks (if any)
- Registration type (the decision is jointly taken by the adopter and the breeder)
- Date of transfer
- Personal information of the breeder including name, address and certifications (if any)
- Information about the new owner
- Signatures of the breeder and the buyer
- Call name of the dog (if any)

The application form is then submitted for approval to registration organizations (like the AKC). Registration fees depend on the type of the registration the owner is opting for. However, usually the registration fees are nonrefundable. If you are buying the puppy from a shelter or a pet store owned by two or more owners, then each owner has to sign the registration form. All the information must be accurate otherwise it will delay the registration process.

In case you are buying the puppy via a third party, you need to attach a supplemental transfer statement with the application form. After the application form is submitted, it will take a few days to complete the registration process. After all the legal work is completed, the registration certificate stamped by the AKC (or the respective authority of the country the buyer belongs to) is mailed to the dog owner. Examine the certificate carefully and in case of any error, contact the registration authority to correct the mistake and reissue the certificate.

In case you lost the registration certificate, contact the breeder and request them to fill out the duplicate form. The breeder will apply for a duplicate registration certificate and you will receive the duplicate copy within a few days.

13. Decision to Buy

Now that you have learnt all about the registration process, it's time to move on to some other important factors that might influence your decision. Dogs make a lifetime companion, so you should make your decision very carefully. Other than health and pedigree, there are several other important factors that you need to consider while purchasing the Finnish Spitz dog.

Here are a few to get you started with streamlining your options and making the final purchase:

How Many Puppies Do You Want?

If you live alone then you might want to buy two puppies to give your pets some company. But there are a few considerations that you must keep in mind if you are planning on buying more than one puppy. The most important factor that can influence your decision is how spacious your house is. The Finish Spitz needs a good, open space to do exercise and physical training. If you don't have a backyard or garden, you can't accommodate more than one Finnish Spitz in your house. In addition, this breed has a very high-pitched voice and it barks a lot. A group of Finnish Spitz can make your house really noisy and it can bother you.

The Best Age for Adoption

The best age for buying a Finnish Spitz is when it's young. Although it is a very adaptable breed and it can easily adjust to you and your family, training an adult Finnish Spitz is a bit difficult. Plus, if you don't have any prior experience of handling a dog, it is recommended for you to get a small puppy that you can handle with ease. Being a hunter breeder, they might behave a little wildly sometimes and if you have not trained it since the beginning, its hunter instincts might scare you. The Finnish Spitz is a very quick leaner and once you have taught it something it will never forget it. So training a previously trained Finnish Spitz is a very challenging task.

Another advantage of buying and raising a young puppy is that you will get a chance to spend more time with it. It will help you understand the eating habits and training needs of the puppy. Particularly if you have other pets and children at your house, the best age to buy a Finnish Spitz is when its 2-3 months old.

Chapter 7: Time to Welcome the Pet

Now that you have decided to bring a Finnish Spitz, it's time to puppy proof your house and make it safe for your new friend and learn about its food and shelter needs. In this section you will find details on the subject, so keep reading.

1. Start with Puppy Proofing

Finnish Spitz dogs are generally very curious and just like small babies they put literally everything to their mouths. You will be astounded by its curious nature and its ability to chew on anything and everything. Keeping their habit to swallow small things in mind, the first thing you need to do is to keep harmful and small things away from their reach.

Dogs have an amazing sense of smell and they are attracted to everything that has a sharp smell (regardless of the type of smell). From leather shoes to perfumes, they are attracted to everything that has a distinctive and detectable fragrance. So make sure you keep all such items like perfumes, laundry, medicines, garbage and chemicals in closets and out of your pet's reach. Don't use normal trashcans for disposing garbage, instead use cans with locking lids. Small puppies love playing with papers, tissues and every other easy-to-shred thing, so make sure you keep all tables and counters clean and free from temptations. Oh and don't make the mistake of giving the puppy your old and useless pair of socks or shoes to chew. Although it will keep the pet happy and busy, it will then chew every shoe or sock it sees- so better not take the risk.

An infant Finnish Spitz is very small in size and can get crushed under heavy decoration pieces. So before bringing your small friend home, secure all dangerous and heavy items (like large vases, cardboards, marble slabs etc.) that can fall on the puppy. Taking care of a small puppy is just like taking care of a crawling baby. You have to keep delicate and breakable items like glass decoration pieces out of their way- otherwise they can hurt themselves. Small Finnish Spitz puppies are very curious to learn about new things- they will inspect everything by touching and licking. So keep shape blades, instruments and pointed things that can hurt the pup locked.

If you think that dog proofing your house is all about picking up things and keeping them locked then that's not all. Put yourself in your pet's shoes and inspect your house with its eye view. Look under furniture and in small corners to see things that can catch your pet's eye and interest. It is really important for you to understand the psychology of your pet to make your house is a safe place for it to live in.

You need to inspect your house for urgent repairs like broken windows and nonfunctional locks to puppy proof your house. Also make sure there is no bad wiring in the house. Wrap the cables and cords of electrical equipment. Puppies have a habit of sniffing around and small holes instantly grab their attention. To keep your pet away from licking or touching electrical sockets, coat them with some bitter and citrus chemical (make sure its non-alcoholic and the dog is not allergic to it) because puppies don't like bitter tastes. You can also cover cords with aluminum foil, as puppies don't like to nibble shiny wrappers.

Small puppies literally lick everything and anything- from their master to walls. To keep the puppy from licking wall paints, use the bitter chemical coat technique. You can use Bitter Apple to coat walls and wires, as it's easily available and does not impact the shine of wall paint. Plus, the Finish Spitz is also not allergic to Apple Bitter. The technique does not work with all dog breeds, but if you are getting a Finnish Spitz then you are lucky because the Bitter Apple technique really works for them.

It's obvious that you can't empty all your rooms to make your house a safe place for your puppy. So you can install baby gates in your kitchen, bathroom and rooms that are full of "prohibited" items to keep the pet off limits. You can also install baby gates near the staircase if the puppy is too small.

The Finnish Spitz, being a wild breed, does not like to be chained all the time, so keep some areas of your house free where you can leave the dog unleashed. Usually a trained Finnish Spitz does not need supervision, but if you have just brought the puppy home you need to keep a good watch on it. The initial days are very critical for training the dog and setting rules that it will follow throughout its life. Even if a room is safe, the puppy will need someone to watch over it.

It's true that you cannot confine the puppy in a room or cage all the time or keep it leashed. Plus, Finnish Spitz needs physical exercise and if you keep it chained it will impact its health. So, to avoid any mishap or chewing disasters, keep the pet occupied with toys. If you have kids or other pets at home, allow them to interact with the puppy so it gets acquainted to them.

The Finnish Spitz wants to live with the family members, but introducing a crate to the puppy can be an effective way to keep it safe and away from items that can harm it. Feed the puppy in the crate during the initial days to make it feel at home. Oh and never chain the puppy as a punishment for not obeying you. This is the only way you can make the idea of sleeping and eating in the crate friendly for your puppy. The Finnish Spitz has a healthy physique, so make sure that the crate is spacious enough for the dog to lie down and its stretch legs.

If the puppy is younger than six months then it will be easier for you to make it comfortable with the idea of eating and sleeping in its crate. Unlike adult dogs, small puppies need potty breaks every few hours and the initial days are the best times to potty train your dog.

2. Shopping List for Spitz

You will need to get some important supplies to welcome your pet properly. Here is the list of items that you will essentially need to keep a dog:

Collar & Leash

The first thing you need for your pet is a collar and a leash. The collar is important because it holds the identification chip of the dog. A dog identification chip contains important information about the dog that can help you track it if due to any reason the pet gets lost. Plus, the leash is also attached to the collar. The adult and trained dogs don't need a leash, but small pups need one, especially when you take them out for a walk.

You can choose the collar according to your taste but make sure that the collar is adjustable and does not hurt the puppy. Usually nylon collars with two buckles work best for wild and strong dogs like the Finnish Spitz. The collars have a tight grip and don't strangle the pet. To make sure that the collar is not too tight for the dog, place your two fingers in between the collar and dog's neck. You will have to adjust the collar with the age of the dog and keep in mind that the Finnish Spitz grows faster than other dog breeds.

The leash that is attached to the collar should be strong enough to hold a strong dog breed like the Finnish Spitz. The Finnish Spitz is a cool tempered dog, but it is a hunter breed after all and when it becomes wild, it is really tough to control the dog. So the leash must be strong enough for you to control the dog and it should not be longer than 4 feet.

ID Tags or Microchips

Usually these chips are inserted in the neck of the dog and the tags in the collar. These are metal chips (often contained in a plastic cover) and these chips contain basic information about the dog (given by the breeder at the time of registration). The tag also helps the owner keep track of the pet.

There are two options to give your pet its identification- micro-sized traceable chips or simple ID tags or you can simply use both to keep track of your pet. The Finnish Spitz is a wild dog breed, so it's a wise idea to attach an ID tag or insert a microchip in its collar.

A basic ID tag is merely a plastic medallion that you can simply attach to the puppy's collar. It bears basic information about the puppy like its name, its owner's name and contact information. You can add more information about the pet on the ID tag, but your contact number and your pet's name is more than enough to reunite you with your beloved pet in case it gets lost.

A microchip on the other hand, is a small device and can only be used for registered dogs. The chip contains the code of your database. Using this code, any kennel club or rescue group can track the owner of the dog. The microchip can also be inserted in between the shoulder blades of the dog. When any rescue group finds a lost dog without an ID tag, it scans it to detect the microchip. The scanner reads the tracking code and upon entering the code into the database, one can access the contact information of the owner (provided by the owner at the time of registration). In case you change your number or address, don't forget to update your information in the database.

Crates and Containment

You will need a small crate to keep the puppy in during the initial days. The Finnish Spitz does not like to be left isolated in kennels, but it must eat and sleep in the kennel. So to train your dog to live in the kennel, use a crate and small containments from the beginning.

When a crate is introduced to the dog, it might become sad but when used correctly the crate can be an effective way to keep your pet safe and out of harm's way. To make the puppy familiar with the idea of living in the crate, feed the puppy in it. One mistake that most dog owners do is they use crate of containment as a punishment. Don't do this. If you make the crate a comfortable place for the puppy, it will feel safe in it. Try to place the kennel at a place where the dog can feel people's presence around it. Isolation makes dogs sad.

If you want to make the shelter cozy and comfortable for the dog, then make sure that the kennel is spacious. The walls should be strong enough to keep an adult and strong Finnish Spitz dog in it. For small pups, you can simply use a comfortable crate to feed the pup, but adult dogs need large cages.

Oh and don't forget the security gates- the Finnish Spitz is a wild dog and loves to run and play, so secure the kennel with locking gates.

3. Different Types of Dog Crates

There are a variety of dog crates available on the market. These crates are made to suit the different breeds of dog: small, big, heavy, light, and much more. Crates are meant to protect the dog and once your Finnish Spitz is trained to live in it, it will love its new home. That's why the crate you buy for your dog must be comfortable for it. It must be the kind of crate that your dog feels relaxed in. Buying a small sized crate will not make your Finnish Spitz happy. So, make sure that the crate you buy is perfect for your dog.

Wooden Crates

Wooden crates are simple and attractive. These crates look perfect in the house and gel with the interior. These crates are airy and can be customized according to the owner's will.

Car Crates

When you are in the car with your Finnish Spitz, it is extremely important for you to provide safety for your pet. The Finnish Spitz is an active dog that will not stay calm in the car if you leave it in the back seat alone. Car crates are designed for a dog's safety in accidental situations. Moreover, these crates will provide safety for the owner as well. Car crates come in a soft metal body so that they do not harm the dog in accidental situations. These crates are soft and relaxing for the dog, hence there is no chance for your dog to panic. If your dog has a habit of chewing the crates, buy a car crate with vertical bars, which will make it hard for your dog to get hold of it. Moreover, make sure that the floor mat of the crate is slip-free because your dog will be in a moving car and might slip and fall if the crate is slippery.

Heavy-Duty Crates

These are the crates that are specifically designed for destructive and aggressive breeds of dogs. The Finnish Spitz is not a destructive dog. However, it can become destructive if it is not trained to live in a crate. If your Finnish Spitz is destructive, make sure you buy a heavy-duty crate for it.

Soft Crates

Soft crates are becoming popular because they are extremely lightweight, comforting, and easy to move. A soft crate is perfect for a dog that is trained to live in a crate. This type of crate is not suitable for the dogs that chew and become destructive. It is important that you first train your Finnish Spitz and then get a soft crate for it. A wired crate makes many dogs suspicious, nervous, and aggressive. The dogs feel that they are under threat. Hence they start to chew on the wire strings and often hurt themselves. These comfy crates are perfect for dogs of all types, except for the destructive ones. Again, train your dog to live in a crate and then buy a soft crate.

Plastic Crates

Plastic crates are good for dogs that like to sleep under tables and on furniture. These crates are ideal for dogs that have bad chewing habits and are easier to carry. These crates can also be used for airline travelling. However, plastic crates can be suffocation for many dogs. Make sure the plastic crate you buy has open spaces for air to enter. Plastic crates are available in attractive colors.

Crate Covers

A crate cover is an essential crate accessory that provides your dog with complete privacy and protection from weather changes. Crate covers help protect your dog from cold winter breezes and the scorching heat of the sun. These covers work best when travelling with your dog in the car.

4. Important Considerations to make when Choosing a Crate for Your Finnish Spitz

The type of crate you choose depends upon a number of factors. If you are choosing a crate for the car, make sure that your car has enough space to accommodate the crate. Many owners make the mistake of buying big sized crates for their dogs. The dogs in large crates have a lot of room to plan escape and become destructive. The right sized crate is the one in which your Finnish Spitz can stand, turn around, and lie down. Below are some tips to consider before buying a crate for your Finnish Spitz.

- Choose a crate that your dog can fit in.
- The dog should be able to stand, lie, and turn around in the crate.
- Measure the height of your dog to choose a crate that it could fit in.
- The crate should be relaxing for your dog.
- The material of the crate should be right for your dog's type.

- If the dog is destructive or has a chewing habit, do not go for a soft crate.
- Purchase accessories for the crate including crate mats, non-slip mats, and much more.
- Do not buy an extremely huge crate.
- Larger sized crates tend to increase housebreaking problems.

5. Grooming Supplies

The Finnish Spitz is a very gorgeous dog breed, yet it needs a lot of grooming and cleaning. As the dog has a double coat of fur, you will need to put in extra efforts to maintain the original quality of the fur and keep it tidy and shiny. Plus, the puppy will also need regular cleaning and washing as it plays a lot outside and excessive exposure to dust pollution might impact the quality of its fur. In addition, trim the toenails of the dog regularly because the Finnish Spitz loves to cuddle and play with you and its sharp nails can hurt you.

You will need the following grooming supplies to keep your pet in the best condition:

- Nail clippers
- Blow dryer
- Towels
- Bristle brush
- Styptic powder
- Comb
- Slicker brush
- Conditioning spray
- Toothbrush and dog toothpaste
- Cotton balls
- Shampoo and conditioner
- Ear cleaning solution
- Scissors
- Grooming table or grooming area

Store the above-mentioned grooming supplies in a large plastic tote so you can easily find them when you need them.

6. The Basic Kit

You have to be really careful with small puppies. They are curious little creatures and want to inspect everything they see. For obvious reasons, you can't be with your pet all the time and it may hurt itself accidently. If your puppy gets hurt then there is no need to panic. That's not such a big deal- but what's important is that you take care of the puppy properly and give it immediate aid. For that you will need a first aid kit and the kit should contain the following supplies:

- Hypoallergenic Adhesive Tape
- Thermometer
- Non-Latex Gloves
- Rolled Gauze
- Water-based lubricant
- Scissors
- Topical Antibiotic Ointment
- Cotton Balls/pads
- Tweezers
- Antibacterial Cleanser
- Syringe – for baby dose
- Instant Cold Pack
- Styptic Powder

Disaster Kit

When you bring a dog home it becomes one of your family members. So another necessity you need to keep for a dog (or any pet) is a disaster kit. Obviously you can't prevent any disaster but what you can do is prepare yourself to fight it and reduce the intensity of damage. Disasters like earthquakes, thunderstorms and fire breakouts can occur at any moment and to keep your pet safe and sound you will need a disaster backpack.

The backpack will contain the following supplies:

- A first aid kit for the pet
- A Disaster Plan- this plan will contain all the tips and guidelines that you must follow during any disastrous situation to keep your family and your pet protected and safe.
- Bottled water that can last at least 3-7 days

60

- A portable Kennel for Emergency Transport
- Shelf Stable Food that can last a minimum 3-7 days
- Pet Rescue Alert Stickers
- Extra Collar & Leash
- Manual Can Opener
- Extra Blanket
- Food/Water Dishes
- Garbage Bags

Dog Bed

A spacious crate is not enough to make it comfortable and cozy for the puppy. You will need a dog bed to give the little fluffy fellow something comfortable to lay its head on. As sleeping in crates or a shelter is something the Finnish Spitz does not like, you will have to put in extra efforts to make the crate a warm and comfortable den for your pet. If the puppy is younger than six months old, you will have to keep it warm at night and a dog bed can do that. However, there is one danger in using normal foam dog beds- stuff like foam and sponges is quite tempting for dogs, and chewing on bedding can cause intestinal blockages or chocking. So, cover the bedding with a towel or blanket.

After your puppy is trained and big enough to sleep on a real bed, you can replace those small crate dog beds with a wide range of cushions, couches and pillows. There are even foam mattresses for dogs because dogs love to lay and stretch on soft mattresses when they are tired. You will have to change the bedding after every month, as the Finnish Spitz shed heavily- but if you are concerned about environmental sustainability, you can use the dog beds that come with biodegradable stuffing.

Food and Water Bowls

A number of pet owners don't include food and water bowls in their pet shopping list, but unlike other pets, you cannot serve dog food in "any" bowl. Dogs, particularly the Finnish Spitz, are naturally susceptible to digestive tract disorders and unhygienic or low quality serving bowls can upset their stomachs. For example if you are using steel bowls, make sure that its stainless steel. Rust or metal particles can trigger allergies in dogs.

Your puppy will need food and water bowls when he/she comes home, and there are many varieties available through your pet specialty retailer. You can choose ceramic or stainless steel dishes, plastic crocks, and even glass bowls — but all these place settings for your pooch have their benefits and drawbacks.

Ceramic bowls, on the other hand, are easier to clean. However, they are breakable and small pups love to play with their food bowls while eating. But don't worry, as ceramic bowls are too heavy to become toys. Stainless steel bowls are also a good option, as they are less expensive than ceramic bowls and last longer.

Food & Treats

If you think that you can buy food and treats later after bringing the puppy home then think again- the pup might seem little but it has a big appetite. Especially the Finnish Spitz puppies younger than a few weeks old have big calorie demands. It's their growing phase and they need proper and healthy nutrition for the development of their bones, fur and internal organs. As the pet's owner, it is your responsibility to take care of the dietary needs of the puppy. During the initial days, it will be difficult for you to understand the portion size and feeding time- but you can consult a vet to become familiar with the nutritional needs of your pet.

There are certain types of food items the Finnish Spitz is allergic to, which you will learn more about later.

Toys

The Finnish Spitz is not a difficult breed to handle, but it wants one thing from you- lots of time. For obvious reasons, you can't dedicate all of your time to your dog, but what you can do to keep it happy is give it interesting toys to play with. It will also keep it busy, thus reducing the risk of chewing disasters. There are different types of pet toys to satisfy the various needs of the dog. For example, there are chew toys like rubber or sponge balls you can give your pet to gnaw on. Then there are stuffed toys the Finnish Spitz can cuddle with. Dogs love fetching games and you can use fetching discs and balls to play with your pet.

You can also use toys to clean and groom your pet. There are tugging toys that help you floss your pet's teeth while it plays. Then there are toys that can enhance the thinking and learning abilities of the pet. Although the Finnish Spitz is a very intelligent dog breed and it's really easy to teach it new things, you can use dispensing devices (a device that releases rewards when the dog accomplishes something) to encourage the pet to do better in future.

7. Food and Shelter

As far as shelter is concerned, the Finnish Spitz will not give you a hard time in living in its crate. However, unlike other hunting breeds, the Finnish Spitz likes to live with its mates and other family members. It likes to be treated as a part of the family, so make sure that you use the crate only as a sleeping place for your Finnish Spitz dog. However, there are some considerations that you must keep in mind when choosing a shelter for the Finnish Spitz dog:

- If you want to make the shelter cozy and comfortable for the dog, then make sure that the kennel is spacious.
- For small pups, you can simply use a comfortable crate to feed the pup, but adult dogs need large cages.
- Try to place the kennel at a place where the dog can feel people's presence around it. Isolation makes dogs sad.
- As the Finnish Spitz is a wild dog and loves to run and play, secure the kennel with locking gates.

Then comes another important aspect- food. If you are a first-time owner, you must be concerned about what to feed your dog, how many times and what should be the portion size. Well, when it comes to food, the Finnish Spitz is a very easy dog to handle. It's not choosy at all but just like every other dog breed, the Finnish Spitz is also allergic to some food items. Good quality food mixed with a little canned food is a balanced combination for the Finnish Spitz. It fulfills all the dietary requirements of the Finnish Spitz. The Finnish Spitz is fond of raw vegetables, fruits and cheese, but you should not allow the dog to eat too much of these food items. For puppies younger than six months, any good quality puppy food will do, but make sure that the brand is reliable. The Finnish Spitz is naturally prone to joint diseases and people food can accelerate calcium loss in their bones, so make sure that you don't feed your dog regular food. The Finnish Spitz does extensive physical exercise, so it is very important that you keep it hydrated. Also make sure to keep the serving bowl clean, as the breed has a very sensitive digestive tract.

The serving size and dietary needs, however, vary with the age of the dog:

- If the Finnish Spitz dog is between 8-10 weeks then feed it four bowls of food every day.
- If the Finnish Spitz puppy is younger than 6 months, the feed it thrice a day.
- If the puppy is a year old, then feed it tow bowls of food every day.
- After a year, one medium bowl of dog food daily is adequate to fulfill the dietary needs.
- An adult Finnish Spitz, however, might ask for food after exercise or a training session, but feeding them excessively can impact their stamina and overall health. So what you can do is break the meal in two portions.

Chapter 8: The First Few Days

The best time to train the Finnish Spitz dog and tame its hunter instincts is when it's young. The breed has a natural ability to learn things quickly, but there are habits like sleeping in a crate or kennel, eating from a bowl and behaving gently that you can only develop when the dog is young and in its learning phase. Plus, when training a Finnish Spitz, you must keep in mind that training a grown Finnish Spitz is far different than training an infant Finnish Spitz pup.

In the beginning you might find it hard to communicate with the puppy, but once the pup starts understanding you, you can train it the way you like. Here in this section you learn in detail all the aspects of training a Finnish Spitz pup.

1. Initial Training

It might sound quite simple and easy, but it's actually the toughest phase of dog training. The initial days are the most important time to make the dog a part of your family and make it familiar with the new environment. Initial training not only includes food and potty training but it also includes a number of other important aspects that you are about to learn.

First Things First

Before starting the proper training session, there a few things that you must get right first. If the puppy is a few weeks old, then you can't potty train it, but what you can do is set a routine for the pup. Set a feeding routine and feed it at the same time every day. Plus, fix a place to feed the puppy, so he/she knows that it can't move the food and water bowl from its place. This is the best way to teach the dog discipline.

Also set a sleeping routine for the pup. Put it in its crate and on the bed at the same time every day. His way it will know its time and place to sleep. If the puppy is used to following a schedule, it will not be difficult for you to potty train it.

The way you teach the puppy also matters a great deal. Rewards always work better than punishments. If you use the kennel or crate as a punishment for the dog for not following you, it will become stubborn. However, if you reward the pet with some toy or food for sleeping and eating in the crate, it will learn to obey and respect you. Of all breeds, the Finnish Spitz is the toughest one to give crate training to, but if you do it the right way, it will not be that difficult. The key is to make a good connection with your dog and try to understand it.

Teach the Puppy Keywords

If you want your dog to understand and follow your commands, then teach it keywords when it's young. The puppy should not only become familiar with the sound of these keywords, but also understand the meaning. The two most important words that a puppy must know and understand are: "No" and "Good." The puppy should know that it must stop doing what it's doing when you say NO. Scold him gently while saying NO so it understands that it's a command to forbid something. And when you say GOOD tap the pup or hug it to make it understand that you are pleased with it.

This training must start when the puppy is 2-3 months old. Your tone and body language also matter. Dogs are very keen observers and they instantly sense if their master is not pleased with them. So be a little strict and use a firm tone when teaching the puppy the meaning of NO. You have to be really patient when teaching the puppy verbal commands. This is a whole new concept for the pups to learn. It's just like teaching a child to speak. Keep practicing it with the puppy until it gets used to it. And don't confuse the dog by teaching too many words or using multiple terms for the same action. For example, if you want to stop the puppy from doing something, stick to "NO".

Don't use any other word than NO like "STOP" or "DON'T."

Clicker Training

To train your Finnish Spitz effectively, it is possible to adopt the 'clicker training' method. The Finnish Spitz is an intelligent and clever dog that picks up different tricks, commands, and voice signals. However, some dogs are trickier and more challenging to train. These dogs require extra-ordinary training methods just like 'clicker training'.

Clicker training means training your Finnish Spitz to follow your commands by the sound of a 'click'. This clicking sound has proved to be extremely effective in training dogs and many expert trainers adopt this method too. The clicking sound that comes from the clicker is distinct and loud, which makes it easier for the dog to listen in chaos as well.

During the training process, the biggest mistake that owners make is to change the words and commands, which makes it confusing for the dog. The dog learns commands that are associated to a certain action and only follows them if they are repeated several times. For example, if you tell your dog 'No' one time and use 'Stop' the other, it will not be able to establish a connection between the voice signals. It will get confused, which will make it harder for it to learn anything at all. However, a clicker makes a high-frequency clicking sound that remains constant.

The clicker training method is a positive reinforcement strategy for the Finnish Spitz. The clicking sound indicates a reward and whenever your dog listens to you, you click and reward. This way the dog forms a strong association between the clicking sound and a reward.

Make sure that you click the clicker when your dog obeys your command or listens to you. Marking bad behavior with the clicker will only create confusions in your dog's mind.

Example:

If you want your dog to sit, use the verbal command 'sit. Have the clicker in your hand and as soon as your dog sits, you click and offer it a treat.

You need to click immediately after your dog obeys your command. If you take too long to click, the dog will get confused.

To train your Finnish Spitz using a clicker, you will need to be patient, consistent, and repetitive. The Finnish Spitz will not pick up this clicker method quickly. Give time to your dog so that it learns how the clicker works.

How does the Clicker Work?

Below are some useful tips to train your dog using a clicker:

- Make the clicking sound only when your dog follows your command the right way.
- Do not take too long to click.
- Clicker training involves a lot of delicious treats for your dog.
- In the initial days of clicker training, offer treats after every success.
- When your dog learns the method, replace treats with toys, hug, snuggle, or pat on the back.
- Feed small sized treats so that your Finnish Spitz doesn't get fat.
- Use hand and verbal actions while training your dog with the clicker.
- Make your dog learn a single command by repeating it several times, so that your dog learns quickly.

Biscuit Training Is Not a Good Idea

When it comes to teaching the puppy by giving rewards, a number of us confuse the word rewards with food. Treating the puppy for behaving well or obeying you does not work always. It might work if the puppy is hungry or the treat is really tempting, but if it's not hungry, it will not really care about the reward and continue doing what it's doing. However, if you teach the puppy to follow your commands and treat them with toys, cuddles and hugs- it will always listen to you.

The Finish Spitz is a very outgoing and adventure-loving dog and it's very rare that the dog prefers a food treat over running wildly, unless the dog is really hungry. So to handle such dogs, you will have to use different tactics other than biscuit training. Use toys and a bonus session of physical training instead, as a reward for the dog to listen to you.

Another thing you must keep in mind is NEVER leave a Finnish Spitz dog unleashed and without collar when taking him for physical training. The hunter breed runs very fast, and if it goes wild it will be really difficult for you to catch up with it. Use a collar and leash from the very beginning, so the puppy gets used to it.

Respect Training Is a Must

You can't teach a dog (particularly a hunter dog like the Finnish Spitz) to obey you, unless it respects you- so respect training is a vital part of dog training and you can only develop a habit of respecting the owner in a dog when its young. Identify yourself as the leader of the house and master. It's true that dogs make the most loyal companions, but it doesn't necessarily mean that they respect you.

One tactic that works in giving the Finnish Spitz respect training is to be friendly with it and respect it. Respect is a game of give and take (even in the case of dogs). Don't tease or hurt your pet. Treat it like your family member and it will respect you. Spend quality time with it, play with it and give warm hugs to show affection and care. All a dog wants is love from its master to stay loyal for life.

Treat the dog for learning something new and obeying you and always call it by its name. One thing you must learn about the Finnish Spitz is it's a very friendly breed but it considers only one person its master and does not allow any other to rule or dictate it.

Crate Training

The best time to let a dog get acquainted with the idea of sleeping and eating in crates or containers is when its 2-3 months old. As the breed is used to living in wide-open areas, it does not like being confined in a small container, but you have to play smart to make your pet like its crate or container.

First of all the choice of container matters a great deal. Choose a spacious crate where the puppy does not feel suffocated. Then make it comfy and cozy by using soft bedding for the puppy to sleep and rest. Set a fixed time and out the puppy on its crate at the same time every night.

The Finnish Spitz are good at following routines- if you teach them to follow a definite schedule from the beginning, they will follow it all their lives. Also, treat your pet with toys and hugs for sleeping in the crate and obeying you.

Acceptance Training

The most important aspect of training a pet is making it accept you as its master or leader. As mentioned above, the Finnish Spitz only obeys its master- anyone who it does not consider its owner cannot give commands (even if the dog is familiar to that person). Unlike adult digs, it's really easy to give small pups (2-3 months old) acceptance training.

To make a connection with the dog, spend as much time as you can with it during the initial days. It's the master who must feed the puppy and take it to exercise. Unlike other pets that get trained by any person- training a dog is tricky. Only one person (the master) can train the dog.

So, as the master of the dog, you must interact with the pet most of the time. Once the acceptance training is over, other family members can spend as much time with the pet as they want- but before that, it's better that only the master should deal with the pet. Usually the acceptance training period lasts for 1 month (for infant pups). If you are worried about the social behavior of the Finnish Spitz, then don't worry- the breed is very friendly and easily adjusts to other people.

Housebreaking Training

Despite being a wild dog, the Finnish Spitz is not destructive and can easily be trained. During the initial days, you have to keep your rooms free of all breakable and delicate stuff. Although the breed is fond of chewing on everything it sees, it does not break things until it trips on anything accidentally. So, for the sake of the puppy's safety and housebreaking training, keep every breakable item in your house, out of the dog's reach.

Also set limits for the dog beyond which it can't go, but for that first teach the pup to follow basic commands.

Gentleness Training

The Finnish Spitz is a very playful and perfect-for-adoption breed, but it's a hunter breed after all. So it's very important that you give your dog gentleness training when it's young. Don't let the puppy bite or clutch you hard, even if it's playing with you. Discourage any wild behavior and be gentle with it. Regularly trim your pets' toenails, because the Finnish Spitz has a very strong grip and even a friendly cuddle can hurt you if you don't keep its nails trimmed.

2. Potty Train Your Dog

Next comes the trickiest phase of training a dog- potty training. If done in the right way, potty training is not as difficult as it seems. Before moving on to the proper training session, let's get on board with the basics of potty training. Whether you are training a small Finnish Spitz puppy or an adult Finnish Spitz, there are a few things that you must keep in mind:

The most important aspect of potty training is understanding your pet. You must be able to understand its body language and read the signs that tell that the pet wants to excrete.

You must know how frequently your pet needs to eliminate. The frequency and intervals vary with their age. Small puppies, for example, excrete more often than adult dogs (that's because small puppies have a bigger appetite and their metabolism works faster than adult dogs).

Once you know the potty timings of your pet, take it outside (to a walk in the backyard maybe) every day at the same time, so he gets used to answering nature's call outside the house.

The best way to teach a dog something is by encouraging them and treating them with rewards. Praise your pet each time it excretes at the right place. Rewarding will ensure the pet that it has done the right thing and it will continue doing it to get its reward from you.

Once the puppy is big enough to understand hand signals, give it signal training. Point in the direction where you want your pet to eliminate. If you keep your door locked, hang a small bell there that will ring when the pet pats the door and you will know that the dog wants to go out to do its business.

71

The Finnish Spitz likes freedom, however don't let your pet roam around unleashed unless it's fully potty trained. You don't want mess in your house, do you?

Crate training can really help you to potty train your pet. Crate training only works if the puppy is really young (2-3 months old). Unlike cats, dogs don't dig the place where they sleep and eat. So, it will eventually go out to excrete.

If you live in an apartment and don't have a lawn or backyard where you can leave your pet to eliminate, you can use litter pans. Place the litter pan outside your apartment and train the puppy to do its business on the pan.

One thing that you must keep in mind before starting potty training your pet is that punishments don't work in the case of dogs. It will only discourage them and a wild breed like the Finnish Spitz might become stubborn with frequent punishments or threats. Be gentle and polite with your pets and treat them like your own kids.

Don't leave the Finnish Spitz home alone until they are fully potty trained- otherwise be ready to return to an all messed up and soiled home.

Be flexible with your pet - accidents can happen. Although the Finnish Spitz is a very obedient breed and it will not poop anywhere else other than its fixed spot, if does, let it go.

It is common practice in wild dog breeds that they mark their pooping spot by urinating at that place, and they just follow the smell of their urine and poop at the same place every time. If your pet marks any place (within the house) spray some deodorizer to kill the smell.

Last but not least - you have to be patient with your pet. It may take you a while to potty train your Finnish Spitz, but once it's trained, it will never forget the rules set by you. Now that you are familiar with the basics of potty training, let's move on how to potty train a Finnish Spitz. Whether you have bought a small Finnish Spitz puppy or an adult dog home, it needs potty training, but training a puppy is easier than changing the pooping habits of an adult Finnish Spitz. In

72

this section you will learn how potty training a puppy differs from training an adult dog:

Potty Training a Finnish Spitz Puppy

There is no denying the fact that housetraining a puppy, no matter what breed it belongs to, is the most challenging phase of all dog training - particularly if you are training a dog for the first time. Most pet owners think that all it takes to housetrain a puppy is to keep the puppy surrounded by old newspapers and soaking papers- but that's not the case.

A Finnish Spitz puppy (younger than 2-3 months) cannot hold pee or poop for a very long time, as its bladder is not fully developed until the puppy is 6 months old. So during the initial days, you will need to keep a strict check on the puppy. It needs to pee and poop a lot. This is the reason that the Finnish Spitz puppies, younger than 6 months, have a large appetite. They eat, burn calories and excrete.

Take your Finnish Spitz puppy to its designated spot for excreting after every nap, play and meal. The puppy might not excrete immediately so wait until it's done with its business.

Follow the same routine every day, until the puppy develops a habit of pooping outside. And yes- you have to be really patient with your pet!

Potty Training an Adult Finnish Spitz

If the Finnish Spitz is older than a year and you think that it would be easier to potty train an adult dog than a small puppy- then think again. You will have to train the dog from scratch. In fact it is more difficult to change the habits of an adult than developing the habits of a small puppy.

You will have to keep a close eye on the Finnish Spitz dog to note its routine and habits. You might even need to keep a diary to note the timings when it goes out and how many times. This will help you synchronize its poop timings with your routine. If the dog is not trained, you can't leave it home alone. Crate training can also work for adult Finnish Spitz dogs, but you will have to introduce the crate to the dog gradually. Commitment and consistency is the key to train the Finnish Spitz dogs.

3. Set the Rules

Setting the rules is the most important aspect of training your pet and the best time to teach a Finnish Spitz dog to follow the rules set by you is when its young (2-3 months). This is the best time when you can tame the behavior and nature of the Finnish Spitz dog according to the environment of your house. The dog alone will not just have to adjust in the new environment but you will also have to change a lot of things in your house for the safety of your pet.

To set the rules, start with teaching the pet some keywords like NO and GOOD and show it the meaning of these words by using rewards. The initial days are crucial for setting the rules and teaching the pet to follow these rules, but once the pet is trained to understand signals and your tone, you can teach it anything.

Chapter 9: Time to Tame and Train Your Pet

After the basic training, it's time to take the training session to the next level. The Finnish Spitz is a wild and aggressive breed and you need to tame their hunter instincts to transform the dog from a hunter wild dog into a domestic breed perfect for adoption. In this section, you will find all the information that can help you start the proper training of your Finnish Spitz dog.

1. Your Pet Needs Training

Training a dog depends on its age and its abilities. If the puppy is younger than 2 months then its learning abilities and requirements are different and for adult Finnish Spitz dogs, the training requirements are different.

A small puppy will take time to understand verbal gestures and hand signals, but if you keep the training sessions slow and easy you can achieve your goals quickly. Just keep one thing in mind - if you expect the puppy to understand you, give it love and take good care of it. This is the best way to bribe a dog to do things that you want it to do.

When you bring a pet home it's a big change for it to cope with. Incorporate with the pet as much as you can and help it make adjustments with the new environment and change its habits and nature accordingly. If the dog is older than 6 months then it will be more difficult for it to change its old habits and adopt new ones. You will have to be really patient around it. A number of pet owners think that training a grown dog is easier as they have a higher intelligence level- but in reality, teaching an adult Finnish Spitz is more challenging. First you will have to work on understanding the old habits of the pet and then teach it new things from scratch.

2. The Basic Training Tips You Need

If you have experience of training dogs, then training a Finnish Spitz dog will not be that challenging for you - but in case you don't have any idea about communicating with the pet and understanding it, then here are some tips that you must keep in mind while training your pet.

Listen To Your Pet

The first and the most important tip to training a Finnish Spitz dog is to make a strong bond with it and that's only possible when you listen to it. If you want the dog to listen to you and follow you then you will also have to understand its need and body language. You should know if your pet is in pain or uncomfortable by reading its body language and making efforts to make it comfortable. Affection and care is all a Finnish Spitz dog expects from its owner to obey him/her.

Show Affection To Your Pet

Your Finnish Spitz cannot read your eyes or can't understand your language, but it can feel the warmth and affection in your gestures. Feed your pet on time, take it for a walk daily, play with it and let your fluffy friend cuddle with you. The Finnish Spitz does not like to be left alone and isolated, so if you are bringing a Finnish Spitz dog home, make sure you give it quality time. Just make your pet fond of you and it will do everything you teach. The Finnish Spitz is not at all a tricky breed to train and tame, if you befriend them.

Know Your Pet's Likes And Dislikes

Yes it's true that the Finnish Spitz is not a choosy breed when it comes to food, but still you should know your pet's preferences in food, treats and toys. This will bring you and your pet closer to each other and this is all you need to train your dog. Observe your pet closely and note what it enjoys and what irritates it. For first-time dog owners, it's understandable to take time.

Tell It That You Are The Boss

This is one thing about the Finnish Spitz dogs- they will be civil with all family members and playful around all familiar faces, but they only listen to their master. You will have to tell your dog that you are the boss and you will tell it what to do. To identify yourself as the leader, spend as much time as you can with the dog during the initial days. Do all its chores yourself, feed it, put it in the crate and play with it. Once the pet starts considering you its leader, it will start listening to you.

Consistency Is the Key

Training a dog is just like teaching a kid something from scratch. You have to be really patient and consistent. You need to do one thing several times to teach your pet, so make sure you have a lot of stamina and tolerance when you start training your dog. They will take time to get acquainted to your signals and language and you must give them enough time and a comfortable environment to learn and grow.

Have Realistic Expectations

Don't overwhelm or scare the puppy with your expectations - don't expect too much from the little fellow. Put yourself in its shoes and think: would it be easy for you to live in a new place, surrounded by unfamiliar faces? Give the puppy enough time to get acquainted with you and the new place and understand the new environment. Help your pet make adjustments with the new environment and change its habits and nature accordingly. For example, the Finnish Spitz is a hunting breed and barks a lot. You can't expect the dog to stop barking just like that. You will have to train it using different techniques and give it a fair amount of time to change its old habits. Young puppies (2-3 months old) will take less time to get adjusted in the new environment, but if the puppy is older than a year, you will have to cooperate with it to learn new things and forget old ones.

Give the Pet High Quality Food

Don't save your money on your pet's food. After all the hard work, your pet needs some high quality treats. Plus, the Finnish Spitz has a very sensitive digestive tract. If fed poor quality food, their stomach will get upset. Another benefit of feeding your Finnish Spitz dog good quality food is that it will increase their stamina and enhance their learning skills. So, if you want your pet to become intelligent and understand you more quickly, feed it good food.

Motivate Your Pet

Encouraging the pet is really important to teach it new things and train it. It will also encourage the pet to do better in the future. Keep in mind that punishments never work in pet training. If the pet does not do something right on the first go, give it another chance and never discourage it by talking it in harsh tone. Rather, pat the dog gently for at least giving it a try. But when the dog does what you want, give it some gift to ensure it that this time it has done the right thing. Don't overwhelm the pet by teaching too many things at the same time. Take the training session really slow paced.

Bribery vs. Reward

You must understand the difference between bribery and reward while training a dog. A reward is a way to encourage the pet to do better in future, but when you bribe the pet to do something, then it will only perform a task when you bribe it. On the other hand, rewarding the pet with its favorite treat for doing a good job is a whole different concept. Treats and rewards enforce a positive motivation in the pet and boosts its moral. It's a really effective way to encourage them to perform tasks beyond its capabilities.

Freedom

Last but not least is freedom. The Finnish Spitz is a hunter breed - it does not like to be chained up all the time. So give it enough space and freedom so that it does not feel suffocated. This breed does not have any specific food requirements, but it definitely needs a lot of physical training and exercise. Take your Finnish Spitz dog outside daily for a walk and when it learns something new or accomplishes something, give it a bonus playtime. With a smart breed like the Finnish Spitz, you will have to play clever and tactics like these always work. But again, consistency is the key to success when it comes to training a Finnish Spitz dog.

3. Get the Pet Accustomed to the Leash

Leash training is another important aspect of early training that can save you from frustration and makes it easier for you to handle your pet when it's all grown. Usually dog owners don't see the need for leash training when the dog is small- but actually that's the best time to leash train your pet.

For a strong and hyper dog like the Finnish Spitz, leash training is a must. Just imagine how frustrating it would be when you take your Finnish Spitz on a walk and it starts pulling you down the sidewalk.

Not only for you, but this can also be bothering for other people walking along the road. If you try to leash your dog then, it will give you a real hard time. So why make it difficult when leash training at a younger age can save you from all the hassle?

The Finnish Spitz is a very active breed and loves walking and physical training. They often become very hyper out of excitement when you take them out for exercise. The Finnish Spitz is a really smart breed - if you have put a leash on your pet before taking it out for walk, then it will know the meaning of putting on the leash. It might get out of control the next time you put the leash on it.

So, to begin the leash training, start to put the leash next to the dog's bowl when it eats so that it associates it with pleasure or happiness. The dog will also get accustomed to the leash if it sees it all the time.

You must also teach the dog to stay calm when you go out. You can't put the leash on just like that and expect your pet to get acquainted to it. For obvious reasons, the pet will try to free itself from the leash, but you have to keep it calmed. Pat the dog gently to calm his nerves down and make it feel better. In fact it will be more convenient to handle your pet if it understands hand signals. You will learn how to teach your Finnish Spitz dog to read hand signals later in the book.

The dog should at least know to sit and stay when you command it to. Don't start the leash training session until the pet is able to interpret the basic commands. It is really important to put a leash on the dog with convenience.

The next step after teaching the dog to sit still while you are putting the leash on it is gaining the control of your hyperactive companion. The Finnish Spitz dog is smart enough to figure out that you are about to take it out - so after you have leashed your dog, it will become super excited and run towards the door. Hold the leash and don't let the pet get out of control. Don't take it out until the dog is relaxed and in control. This way the pet will soon learn that the walk will not begin until it calms down.

When the dog calms down, praise it for obeying you (a gentle pat will do) and then take it out for the "much anticipated" walk. If the pet pulls on the leash and tries to run, hold the leash and stop then and there. Don't move until the pet stands still - this way the dog will learn that it is not supposed to pull the leash and run away from its master.

4. Walking Training

Once your Finnish Spitz is used to wearing the leash and following your commands, you can take it with you in crowded areas like parks and roads (with the leash on of course). But if you take care of a few minor concerns, walking sessions will become fun for both you and your pet. Start with deciding which side (left or right) works best for you. For example, if you are right-handed, you might want to keep the pet on the right side. When the pet is on the correct side, start walking but make sure you walk at a slow place, at least during the initial days of leash training. Keep the dog close to you as you walk to keep a check on it. You might need to synchronize your pet's walking pace with yours by holding the leash, but soon the pet will know that it has to accompany its master.

Nothing (in pet training) happens overnight. You will have to work hard and sit patiently to see the desired results. Continue the leashed walking sessions with consistency until the dog learns to stay on the designated side and walk with you. Praising the pet and treating it with rewards will encourage it to perform even better in future. The reward also ensures the pet that it has done the right thing and his master is happy with him!

Usually the right handed people prefer to keep the dog on their right, while left handed people are comfortable with keeping the dog on their left. But there are a number of theories as to which side the pet should walk on. Have a look at some of these theories about walking position:

- If you are walking along a road or street, the dog should be away from the street. This position will help you keep your dog from blocking traffic or people.
- The Finnish Spitz was originally bred by hunters and they used to keep it on their left side while walking. This is because hunters usually carry hunting weapons on their right shoulder.

80

- You can also train the dog to stride from one side to another. In case you have two pets, you can keep one pet on each side.

Don't let Your Finnish Spitz Pull on the Leash

Training your Finnish Spitz to walk on the leash is not an easy job. It requires a lot of patience and consistency. The Finnish Spitz is naturally very active. They like to run and explore their surroundings and that's the reason they pull on the leash and drag their owners along.

The Finnish Spitz's natural instincts tell it to run and explore. To make this habit go away, you have to be very vigilant in its leash training process. Many Finnish Spitz dogs pull on the leash because they think that they are leading their owners. However, you have to be in control of your dog to make it understand that it cannot lead you anywhere; instead, you are the boss. Becoming the boss of your dog means ample respect and obedience training. Once your dog sees you as the authority, it will never try to pull on the leash.

Below are a few tips for the Finnish Spitz owners to make 'pulling on the leash' stop:

- When your Finnish Spitz pulls, stand still and do not move. This will tell the dog that you are not interested in moving in the direction it wants you to move. This will also prove to your dog that you are in charge of its actions and movements.
- When your leash loosens, apply a little force and move in another direction so that your Finnish Spitz cannot pull in the direction it wants to.
- Another way of making the pulling stop is to walk in the opposite direction. When you walk in the opposite direction, your dog will get the message that you are the authority and the dog moves in the direction you want it to move.
- Use the clicker training method to leash train your dog and to put a stop to its pulling habits. Use the clicker when your dog stops pulling and reward. You may also tell your dog to stop and use the clicker for that command. Once your dog stops and starts moving with you, offer a treat so that it learns the trick.

81

- Make sure you keep your dog on your left side and make it walk at your pace. Offer treats whenever your dog behaves and walks properly.
- Do not stop training the dog until it stops pulling on the leash.
- Keep training your dog to walk on the leash until it has reached perfection.
- Do not pull on the leash too hard as it may suffocate the dog or hurt its sensitive neck.

5. Maintaining Your Patience with the Pet

The initial days are not only difficult for the pet, but they are equally difficult for the owner as well, particularly if the owner does not have prior experience of adopting dogs. Now that you have brought your little companion home, it is your responsibility to take care of it and consider it a part of your family. Just like the dog needs training to adjust with you and your family, you also need to maintain patience with the pet.

The cute little fellow is not a toy; it is a living being and needs as much affection and care as any human baby would need. Give your dog the love and attention it expects from you and it will always stay loyal and obedient to you. You just have to be consistent with it, put in your best efforts and give the pet a lot of time. Once you have developed the bond with it, it will be easier for you and for the pet to understand and communicate with each other.

6. Teaching Hand Signals

It is really wise to teach your pet to interpret hand signals along with following verbal commands. A dog, for obvious reasons, cannot understand your language, so it will take it longer to get used to verbal commands compared to learning hand gestures. Dogs are naturally skilled at reading and understanding body language and tone. They are keen observers and quick learners- so interpreting hand signals is not that big of a deal for them. All they need is practice and regular lessons.

A dog that is able to understand and follow verbal commands and hand signals is definitely better off than the one who can only do one of these tasks. Plus, the Finnish Spitz has exceptional sight. They can pick up your hand signals from distance. Another advantage of teaching your dog hand signals is that it's a universal language. When it comes to verbal commands, every dog owner has its own keywords. For example, there can be multiple keywords for stopping the dog from doing something like NO or STOP, but there is only one hand gesture for STOP. So, in case you need someone to supervise your pet in your absence, you won't have to give them the list of commands that your dog understands.

While you can create hand signals for different tasks, there are some basic commands like sit, stop, come and heel for which there are standard hand gestures. As a dog owner, you must learn these signals and for your convenience. These gestures are demonstrated below:

Sit

- Make your Finnish Spitz dog stand in front of you
- Use one arm (left or right, it's up to you) for signaling and hold the favorite treat of your dog in the same hand in such a way that the treat is visible to the dog.
- While the dog eyes the treat, bring your forearm upwards slowly with the hand holding the treat facing up.
- Move your hand slowly in the upward direction as your dog moves its head up to follow the treat.
- As the dog raises its head, its rear will naturally go down in a sit.
- If the dog tries to jump to get the treat, GENTLY push its hind legs down into a sit position. Do not push too hard.
- When the dog sits down, pat him and give him the reward.

Lie Down

- Make your Finnish Spitz dog sit in front of you
- Use one arm for signaling and hold the favorite treat of your dog in the same hand in such a way that the treat is visible to the dog.
- While the dog eyes the treat, extend your forearm straight in front of you with the hand holding the treat facing down.
- Move your hand slowly in the downward direction as your dog moves its head in the direction of the treat.

- Keep lowering the treat until the dog's elbows touch the ground and it is lying down.
- When the dog is in the lying position, pat him and give him the reward.

Stay or Stop

- When your dog has learnt the sit and down signals, it's time to teach it the stop signal.
- Make your Finnish Spitz dog sit or lie in front of you.
- Use one arm for signaling and hold the favorite treat of your dog in the same hand in such a way that the treat is visible to the dog.
- While the dog eyes the treat, move your forearm in the upward direction and open the palm just as someone giving the stop signal.
- Move away from the dog and when it does not follow you, pat him and give him the reward.

Heel

- When you teach the dog to heel, make sure that your dog's shoulder is closely aligned with your knee.
- Tap on your thigh to grab the attention of your dog and signal it to stay with you in the same position.
- Praise the pet as he follows you.

Come

- To teach this signal, move a few feet away from the dog.
- Use one arm for signaling and hold the favorite treat of your dog in the same hand in such a way that the treat is visible to the dog.
- While the dog eyes the treat, bring your forearm upwards slowly with the hand holding the treat facing up.
- Move your hand slowly in the direction of your shoulder.
- The dog will come running to you to fetch the treat.
- As he comes to you, praise him and give him the reward.

The above-mentioned guidelines are for standard signals to help the first-time dog owners teach hand gestures to their dog, but if you have experience of owning and training a dog, you can recreate these signals. The Finnish Spitz has the natural potential to learn signals and commands more quickly than other breeds- you just need to be consistent and patient while training your dog.

Chapter 10: Dealing With the Barking Habit of the Finnish Spitz

When you are bringing a Finnish Spitz dog home, you must be aware of all its habits, pros and cons to prepare your house and yourself. Well, there is no denying the fact that the breed is exceptional in many aspects, but there is one characteristic that might become a trouble for you later - the Finnish Spitz is a barking dog. It has a very high-pitched voice and barks a lot. One way to deal with this excessive barking is install soundproof glass in your house. But this technique won't do for when you leave the dog in the backyard or some open area to play. So what to do to control the barking of the Finish Spitz? Well, you need to train your dog and in this section you will learn how.

1. Know Why Your Dog Is Barking

To solve a problem, you must know the root cause of the problem. Similarly, if you want your dog to bark less, know the reason why it's barking. There are some dog breeds like the German Shepherd that bark to express aggression and anger, while other breeds like the Gray Hound bark for no reason. The Finnish Spitz was originally bred for hunting and it used to inform its master about prey by barking loudly. The breed is perfect for adoption and you can easily train it, but there are some wild instincts that you can't tame, like barking.

But unlike some other breeds, the Finnish Spitz never barks without reason. So if you want to control the barking habit of your pet, find the problem and solve it. There can be a million reasons that can make a Finnish Spitz dog bark like hunger, pain, anger etc. You can only understand the problem if you know your pet well. During the initial days, it will be a little challenging for you to control the barking habit of your Finnish Spitz dog, but as you spend more and more time with your pet, you will become familiar with its habits and temperament.

2. What Can You Do To Control The Barking?

As mentioned earlier, the Finnish Spitz seldom barks without a reason. So the simplest way to deal with its barking habit is to solve the problem that's making your pet bark. However, it's understandable that you might take some time to figure the problem, if it's not obvious. For example, if you have just fed your dog and it's barking uncontrollably, you will need to think of other reasons and this might take you a while. Meanwhile, what you can do to keep your pet calm and relaxed is give it some toy to play with and keep it busy. Even a gentle pat and a warm cuddle would do to calm down the restless nerves of your pet. This is the best thing about dogs - all they need from their owner is a dose of love.

3. Possible Reasons of Barking

There can be a thousand reasons that can make a Finnish Spitz dog bark - they even bark when they are happy and excited. Some reasons are quite evident, like if your dog is barking and it's his mealtime, you might quickly figure out that the dog is hungry. But there are certain reasons that are not too obvious and can't be figured out easily. Here is a look at some of those reasons:

The Finnish Spitz is a family-oriented dog. It does not like to be shut out and left alone. So, if you have left your dog out and it's barking constantly then it wants you to take him inside the house.

This breed gets extremely excited when it sees any small bird or animal and barks to grab the attention of its master. So if you have just taken your pet outside and it has started barking hopelessly, then look out for the bird (or animal) that's making your dog all excited.

Make sure you keep your pet clean and bathe it with an anti-flea shampoo. Fleas can really annoy your pet and to vent out irritation, it will bark. So if you have not taken your pet for a flea and parasite inspection lately, do it now!

The Finnish Spitz does not like to miss its training session. If you don't take your dog on a daily walk or exercise, it will express its anger by barking aggressively. You can easily notice the aggression when the Finnish Spitz is barking in anger.

The Finnish Spitz can also bark if it wants to poop and can't find its way out to the designated spot. If the Finnish Spitz is potty trained, it will never poop or pee in the house.

The Finnish Spitz also barks when it senses some threat and that's why they make great watchdogs. So if your dog is barking at night, it might be trying to make you alert of some intruder.

Last but not least - the Finnish Spitz also barks when it's in pain, but you can sense the restlessness in its voice. So if your dog is barking continuously and you can't find the reason, take it to a vet and get it checked. In fact, make a habit of visiting a vet regularly.

Chapter 11: Time to Move On to Adult Training

Now that you are familiar with the basics of pet training and are all set to welcome your new friend, it's time to move on to the difficult part - the adult training. Well, in truth, if you have given proper attention to the basic training and your pet understands you, you will not find this phase all that difficult and challenging. If you are a first-time dog owner, you might need to work a little harder, but you can totally do it. Just remember, consistency and determination are the key to training a dog.

Before getting on board with the adult training, you must know what is included in the "next-level" training. First of all, let out a sigh of relief that you are done with challenging parts like potty training and teaching your dog to follow hand gestures and verbal commands and then prepare yourself for the new challenge. Adult training includes all these things that will help your dog to live on its own. You can't supervise it all the time (particularly if you work or have kids at home to watch over). So, your pet should know how to take care of itself. In a nutshell, adult training is all the things that would prepare your pet to step into the real world - from leash free training to teaching the dog traffic rules, adult training includes everything.

In this section you will all the information you need to train your Finnish Spitz dog to face new challenges.

1. Behavioral Issues Your Pet Might Face

We generally focus on all types of possible issues our pet might face, but we ignore behavioral issues common in pets, particularly dogs. A dog with behavioral issues can be really difficult to handle and gives their owners quite a difficult time. If not taken care of on time, behavioral problems can become severe and then you will have no choice other than giving away your beloved pet. To avoid such trauma, it's better to learn about common behavioral problems in the Finnish Spitz before bringing it home.

Most behavioral problems can be treated if diagnosed at an early stage, but for that you will have to keep a close eye on your pet. In dogs, isolation, anxiety and depression can lead to common behavioral problems. For example, if you don't socialize your dog properly and encourage it to interact with family members, kids and other animals - it might become mentally disturbed at some point in its life and this will impact its overall behavior. As the owner, it's your responsibility to prepare your pet for all unexpected events in its life and encourage it to interact with the world.

Although behavioral problems are not fatal (in most cases), you might want to know what you should do if your Finnish Spitz is going through some mental or behavioral problems. To know the answer, keep reading.

Aggressive Behavioral Problem

Aggression is probably the most common problem in the Finnish Spitz. The dog either becomes aggressive towards other animals or towards its master, depending on the reason of aggression. This breed is usually friendly towards other pets, but if it feels your attention is divided, it might become jealous of other pets and become really aggressive towards them. The Finnish Spitz is a very obedient breed, but an aggressive Finnish Spitz can be really dangerous.

The aggressive behavioral problem is more common in adult Finnish Spitz than in the younger ones. This is because since an adult Finnish Spitz has spent more time with you, he has already established his own identity and place in the house and when it feels someone is trying to take its place it becomes angry and enraged. It's true that resolving such issues is a little challenging, as you can't give all your time to your Finnish Spitz dog, particularly if you have other pets at home. But what you can do is make your dog feel special by giving it treats, warmth, hugs, and most importantly, quality time. Take it outside daily for walk, play with it, feed it on time and don't make it sleep outside the house in isolation.

Older dogs usually try to overpower other pets to show them that they are the bosses and they run the show - don't let them do so. Be gentle with your Finnish Spitz but don't let it forget that it's you who is the boss, not the dog. As far as his insecurity is concerned, ensure it with your love and care that you have not replaced it with new or other pets.

Aggression in dogs, particularly in a wild breed like the Finnish Spitz, can be really dangerous. It might start with excessive barking, mood swings and appetite loss, but if not taken care of properly, a dog with this behavioral problem can also start biting. And do remember that chaining and isolating the dog will only make the issue worse. There are also vaccinations to calm down and sedate an aggressive dog - if you think you can't handle your pet on your own, take it to a vet.

Separation Anxiety in Dogs

Crate training is very important to teach the dog to eat and sleep in its crate or kennel, but make sure you keep its crate within the house. Chaining the dog outside the house during night is the biggest mistake that pet owners can make. Of all pets, dogs are the most loving and caring and they expect the same from their owner. If you don't give your pet quality time and keep it locked in a cage, it might suffer from separation anxiety. It's true that you can't be with your pet all the time, so what you can do to reduce the risk of this behavioral problem is to socialize your pet when it is young. Allow it to play and interact with other pets and family members. Although the Finnish Spitz only considers one person its master, it likes the presence of people and animals around it.

If your pet is already suffering from separation anxiety, take it to a vet. He/she will give the dog medicines to keep it calm and relaxed so you can enforce positive behavior in your pet. There are canine behavioral consultants who can give you the best advice, after examining your pet and evaluating its mental state.

Coprophagia or Eating Poop Problem

A civil, trained, and healthy Finnish Spitz is very particular about its pooping place. It will never eliminate anywhere else other than its designated spot. But if you ever catch your Finnish Spitz dog eating its poop or sniffing it, your dog might be mentally ill and needs some treatment. Commonly known as Coprophagia, this is another common disorder in dogs in which they become obsessed with the smell and taste of their own poop.

There are a number of reasons that can cause this behavioral problem in dogs, but one of the most common reasons is malnutrition. If your pet is deficient in some nutrient, he might start eating its own poop and this is common in young dogs. Puppies younger than 2 months are developing their internal organs and they need food after every few hours to energize themselves. If you don't feed them properly and on time, they might suffer from Coprophagia.

Some dogs also do this out of habit but luckily the Finnish Spitz is not one of those breeds. If your Finnish Spitz is exhibiting this unusual behavior then there must be a genuine reason for it. Try to figure out the reason and resolve it. Other than feeding quality food to the dog, chew toys can also help. Young puppies need something to chew on all the time and if they can't find anything, they start working on their poop. But you always have the option to help your pet get over this practice and the best age to change a dog's habits is when it's young and in the learning phase. Dogs have an exceptional memory and they seldom forget anything.

Chewing Habit

Dogs love chewing things. Small pups, particularly, chew on anything and everything they see. That's normal behavior. But if you don't civilize your dog when it's young and discourage it when it chews on something, this habit can really become a trouble for you. Nothing in your house will be safe then - from your clothes to important documents. So the best way to tame this behavior of your Finnish Spitz dog is to stop it every time you see him chewing something.

For example, if the dog is chewing on a piece of paper, take it away from it and give him his chew toy. Do this every time to make the pet understand that when it feels like gnawing or chewing, to work on one of its toys. And yes, keep dog toys somewhere your pet can easily reach.

The Finnish Spitz has a very curious nature and wants to explore every new thing on its own, which is not bad but there are things that can harm your pet, for example sharp and pointed objects. One way to protect your pet is keeping all potentially dangerous objects away from its reach (which is obviously not possible). So what you can do is, coat all the items in your house that might grab the interest of your pet and harm it with some bitter chemical (for example organic bitter apple). The Finnish Spitz really doesn't like bitter tastes and it instantly loses interest in things that taste bitter.

Submissive Urination

This might sound a little disturbing, but sometimes dogs urinate submissively to show respect to their master or fellows. This happens when the dog can't think of or does not know any other way to show respect. An over-tamed or excessively punished dog often suffers from submissive urination.

A potty trained Finnish Spitz has a definite schedule and it never excretes other than its fixed times and that's usually after meals and before sleeping. But if your Finnish Spitz is urinating excessively then there can be two possibilities, whether it is suffering from submissive urination disorder or something is wrong with its bladder.

It's usual in young puppies to urinate often, as their bladder is developing and they can't hold it for long but an adult Finnish Spitz only pees when it really needs to. Usually fear of punishment causes submissive urination. If you threaten your pet or scare it with something, it might pee when it can't accomplish any task assigned by you. The only way to resolve this issue is to be friendly and gentle with your dog. Treat it like your own kid and be patient while training it.

When it comes to dogs, particularly sensitive dogs like the Finnish Spitz, treats and rewards work better than punishments. Spend more time with your pet to understand its body language, needs and gestures and train it to communicate with you. Encourage it to boost its moral and self-confidence.

Biting Habit

The Finnish Spitz does not only bite out of aggression and anger. When it does not know how to show affection, it bites and that's not usual - it's an indicator that your pet might be suffering from some kind of emotional disorder. If your Finnish Spitz is suffering from a biting disorder don't discourage it harshly, it will only make the issue worse. Brush it off gently and give warm hugs and cuddles more frequently, so it knows the right way to show love and affection.

Dogs are more sensitive than other animals and hence prone to behavioral problems. So if you catch your dog doing something weird, don't panic - it's not that of a big deal. However, it's important that you give attention to your Finnish Spitz and understand its needs.

Dog behavioral issues are often quite complex and difficult to understand and the worst part is there are no quick fixes for these problems. You will have to work hard and consistently with your dog to overcome these problems.

2. Leash Free Training

You might think what's the point of giving a dog leash-free training when you have already trained it to walk with a leash on? Well, there is always a chance that your dog will sneak out of the house on its own and it's very important for its security that it must know how to walk on the road without a leash on. But giving the leash free training to the pet is, without any doubt, a challenging task - particularly for those who don't have prior experience of training dogs.

If you think that the old-fashioned tactics like scaring the pet or tempting it with a treat would work here too, then think again. You will have to be smart and handle your pet strategically to give it leash free training. Treats and rewards work better than punishments and threats, but in this section you will learn to use "behavior" as treats instead of toys or food. Confused? Just give this section a thorough read to know how you can actually make your pet do what you want without rewards when its off its leash.

Premack Principle - What Is It?

Using behavior as a reward is a method introduced by Dr. David Premack and hence it is named after him. Dr. Premack researched the psychology of dogs and compared it with that of humans. He

94

concluded that just like humans, you can also make a dog work by playing smart. According to this research, there are two types of behavior; one that your dog prefers (more likely) and the other one that you prefer (less likely). You can always reinforce the less likely behavior in your doing by tempting it with the more likely one. A simple example might simplify this for you: you want to go out with your friends (more likely behavior) but your mom wants you to finish your homework (less likely behavior). So instead of forcing you to stay home and study, your mom would ask you to do your homework first so you can go out with your friends and you will happily obey her. So, the key is to use your pet's desires and more likely behaviors as the reward to do what you want it do. The trick really works for off-leash training.

Now apply this training principle on your Finnish Spitz dog. To do so, you must observe your pet closely and note its behavior, interest, likes and dislikes. The Finnish Spitz, being a hunter breed, takes interest in every small and fast moving object (for example small birds, fire hydrants etc.). Your pet can find a number of distractions every time you take it out and you can use these distractions to reinforce positive behavior in your dog. Instead of distracting your dog from whatever excites it, allow it to enjoy it after it follows your commands. This is how the famous Premack principle works for dogs and it is more suitable and practical because if you don't have any treat to offer your dog (like food or toy) it will not obey you.

Controlling a dog with a leash on is easier than without leash, for obvious reasons. You can teach your dog a few important things like what to do when you pull the leash and it's good to accompany you everywhere. But when you start off-leash training, don't take the dog directly to roads or crowded places, even if your dog is trained to follow commands and hands gestures. Although it's very rare that a Finnish Spitz does not respond to your call, it is an animal after all and it might get carried with so many distractions. So to start the off-leash training, develop a habit in your dog to keep checking in with you. You can train your dog to respond to your calls, but what if you are busy talking to someone and forget to call your dog? So, the first step of off-leash training is teaching your dog to check in with you every few minutes, without being called.

The next thing to remember for starting the off-leash training sessions is to grab the attention of your dog. Choose an area of practice that's not "too interesting" for your pet, like the backyard. Take the dog out with its leash, walk a few steps and then stop. Wait for your dog to look at you and as soon as it looks at you, say "GO!" and unclip its leash. You don't need to give your dog any treat as a reward, as it will be happy enough to be set free.

So, that's how you use the desire of your pet to explore and roam around freely as a reward to listening to you. But keep mind that you will have to repeat the same practice daily every time you take the pet out for many weeks until your dog knows that it has to focus on you and wait for your signal to move forward.

Once set free, your dog will be all excited and hyper but you have to keep it calm by keep calling its name and giving commands. Make sure you train your dog to listen to your voice commands and hand signals when it's free and on its own. This is really important for the safety of your dog, particularly when you are on the road or in a crowded place. Keep realistic expectations from your pet; don't overwhelm the little fellow with your expectations. Put in your best works and be consistent, as determination is the key to success when it comes to training a dog.

Why Is Off-Leash Training Important?

Many dog owners think that leaving the dog off-leash is dangerous and hence they don't give their dogs leash-free training, which is wrong. It is true that leaving the dog on its own is not safe practice, particularly if you live in a busy city. But you must prepare your pet for unexpected events too. There can be times when you are not there to protect your dog- so it's your responsibility to teach the dog to live on its own. There is no denying the fact that leaving a dog leash-free increases the risk of accidents and mishaps, but with the right training and management you can reduce the risk to a considerable extent. If your dog is leash trained and familiar with hand gestures and commands, it will be easier for you to give it the leash-free training.

3. Teaching Traffic Rules to your Pet

Now that you have taught your dog to walk safely without a leash on, it's time to teach it basic traffic rules and road sense. Walking training is all about teaching the dog to stay close to you when you take it outside (with or without a leash on) but you must prepare your pet for unexpected events, as mentioned above. For the safety of your pet, you must give it the basic road sense training and traffic rules.

Walking on the Road

The most important aspect of the basic walking training that most dog owners ignore is teaching the dog to only start walking after you signal it. Breeds like the Finnish Spitz become excited when they go and it's really difficult to control them. So make sure you give your dog the basic walking training in a park or some safe area before taking it on the road. Your pet might lose a limb or get seriously injured and you don't want that, do you?

The best and the safest way to avoid accidents is to put the leash on when you are walking on a busy road, but if you forget to do so, obedience and signals training can keep your pet safe. So before you start walking training, work on obedience and hand gestures training.

Who's The Boss?

You can teach anything to your dog if you identify yourself as the BOSS. Pampered pets start considering themselves as the boss and they expect their owners to follow their commands. This not only makes dogs stubborn but it can also be harmful for them, particularly when you are on the road. Teaching your Finnish Spitz dogs to interpret gestures and understand commands is not enough, it's also important that the pet listens to you immediately. You will have to tell your dog that you are the boss and you will tell them what to do.

To identify yourself as the leader, spend as much time as you can with the dog during the initial days. Do all its chores yourself, feed it, put it in the crate and play with it. Once the pet starts considering you as its leader, it will start listening to you.

Use Old Commands

You can control your dog on the road with just two words: "Come" and "Stop". There is no need to teach a lot of keywords and gestures to the dog and confuse it. The Finnish Spitz has an exceptional memory and learns things very quickly but it's a living being in the end. It can confuse the meaning of words too, so use as few commands and gestures to teach your pet road sense as possible.

Leash Control Is Very Important

The best way to avoid accidents is to take your dog with a leash on but it's not easy to control a heavy and aggressive dog like the Finnish Spitz, even with a leash when it's trying to run away from you. This leash control is very important. You will have to give your pet proper leash training to keep it under control. If the dog is not leash trained, it will not understand leash signals. For example, it won't have any idea what are you trying to do by holding the leash back. It will try to pull you or free itself from the leash. But that's what leash training is all about. It not only helps the pet get acquainted with the idea of being leashed, but also makes it familiar with common leash signals.

Give the pet the basic leash training in your backyard or some park and you will have to be really consistent. You can't tame the Finnish Spitz just like that. It was bred to hunt and has wild instincts that wake up the moment it sees any small bird or animal. So leash train the dog in a park where it can come across small animals like squirrels. It will help you practice calming a super excited Finnish Spitz with a leash. When you think your pet is fully leash trained, only then take it out on the road.

Reward Your Dog

Don't forget to reward your dog with its favorite treat for obeying you and behaving well. Rewards ensure dogs that they have done well and they will do it again to get their reward. The best reward for a dog however is a warm hug and love from its master.

4. How to Avoid Accidents While Training

Even if your dog is fully trained and you always put a leash on it when going out, there is always a risk of accidents and mishaps. You can do your best to avoid accidents, but you should know what to do if your pet gets injured. But before moving on to the steps that you should take after an accident, let's have a look at some tips that work for avoiding accidents.

Stay Close To Your Pet

Develop a habit in your pet to keep in check with you. You can do this during the initial phase of leash training. If your dog has a habit of waiting for you after walking every few steps, it will automatically reduce the chances of accidents.

Road Sense

Your dog must have basic road sense. For example, it must be trained enough to evaluate its distance from the car when crossing the road. You can do this by taking your dog with you on the road trips and teach it to cross the road (but make sure you put a leash on your dog).

Don't Lure Your Pet with Food

Training the pet is not enough; training it the right way is more important. You can make a dog do anything if you tempt it with rewards and treats, but that does not mean that your dog is trained. Yes, treats and rewards can help during the initial days when you are teaching your dog to obey you and treat you like the boss. But the same tactic can't work for the next-level adult training. You must not lure your pet with treats and toys to follow your commands when you are teaching it road sense. This is important because the dog will wait for its treat to follow your command; if you don't have anything to offer, it will probably not listen to you. On the other hand, using your pet's interests as a reward is a smarter technique that always works.

Leash Size Matters

Make sure that the length of the leash is not shorter or more than 6 inches. The leash should be long enough to give the dog a sense of freedom when it goes out and at the same time it must allow you to stay close to your pet. Plus, using Swivels also decrease the risk of accidents. Leashes can easily get tangled with your feet and you can tumble upon your own pet. It might not hurt an adult dog, but for a puppy the impact is enough to give it a few fractures and you don't want to do that to your pet. So make sure you use the right kind of leash with swivels, as swivel keeps the leash from tangling.

5. What To Do If Your Dog Gets Into An Accident

Nobody wants to see their dog with nasty injuries and fractured limbs, but it's an animal after all. It does not have road sense like humans and there is always a chance that your pet gets hurt accidentally (even if it's fully trained). If you know the steps that you must take immediately after the accident, you can reduce the impact of the accident to a significant extent.

Start off with giving the dog immediate treatment. Make sure you make a backpack containing emergency supplies like a first aid box and keep the backpack with you whenever you take your dog out for exercise, walk or for playing. If the dog is bleeding, clean the scar with an anti-septic liquid and apply a bandage to stop the bleeding. Then take your pet immediately to a vet and give it proper treatment. There are injuries that are not apparent. If you cannot see it, it does not mean that it does not exist. Your dog obviously can't tell you where it hurts, so make sure you get your dog checked by a professional vet. He/she will run tests to see if there is any internal injury or broken bones.

There is something worse than injuries that can impact the mental and physical health of your dog and this is post-accident trauma or shock. The Finnish Spitz, despite being a wild and hunter breed, is a very sensitive dog breed and with a dog like that you should be very careful. Traumas can even become life threatening for dogs as it can disturb the normal functioning of the heart and blood supply to all parts of the body. This is the reason that your dog immediately needs trauma treatment after it meets an accident. Delaying the treatment can even cost you your pet's life!

Shock or Trauma

When a dog is hit by something with sudden impact like any vehicle, it paralyses its heart for a few seconds and scares it. Some accidents might also cause internal bleeding, which ultimately reduces the amount of blood and a dog might go into shock due to internal injury. This type of trauma is called hypoglycemic shock. It's more dangerous because you can't see the extent of the injury and you might delay the treatment and this can cause irreparable damage to your pet. Hypoglycemic shocks can even damage dogs permanently, but with immediate treatment you can reduce the extent of the damage.

Symptoms of Shock

There are other types of shock too that can impact the overall health, abilities and personality of your pet. For example, some impacts can be so sudden and powerful that they can instantly lead to heart failure. Other shocks that a dog is prone to during accidents is septic shock. The impact of septic shock is not instant as it is caused by infections but if not treated properly it can lead to amputation, removal of the infected organ or even death. So it is really important that you take your pet to a vet for vaccination after any accident or injury. Your dog can also suffer from neurogenic shock that impacts its ability to learn and understand. There are different therapies to get your pet out of the neurogenic shock. Regardless of the type and cause of shock, it is a life-threatening medical state for dogs, so don't take it lightly.

As the medical condition is not apparent, and for first time dog owners it is really difficult to deduce that their pet is in shock, here is a list of common symptoms that you must watch out for in your dog after any accident or injury:

Early Stage Symptoms

- Rapid heartbeat (right after the accident)

- Body temperature drops abnormally and the dog becomes extremely cold
- Anxiety and agitation
- Very weak pulse and can't be located easily
- Bright red gums
- Gums become white (almost colorless) or in some cases, mottled
- Shallow breathing
- Constant low rectal temperature

Middle Stage Symptoms

- Heart beat becomes faster and more abrupt
- Respiration rate is normal but breathing becomes shallow
- Dog becomes week and seems tired all the time
- Pulse is more difficult to locate

Late Stages Symptoms

- Heart rate becomes irregular and rises abnormally sometimes, which can cause the dog's cardio muscles to go weaker and eventually fail.
- The dog becomes even more tired, lazy and eventually slips into a coma
- Change in breathing pattern- becomes heavier
- Respiration becomes rapid and deep
- Eye balls become unfocused
- The eyes appear to glaze

6. Treating a Dog in Trauma

In order to treat your dog and help it recover from the state of shock, it is really important that you are able to read the signs at an early stage. Shock treatment during the early stages of trauma is possible, but as the time passes by the chances of recovery become slimmer. No matter how close you are to your dog and how well you know it, you can always miss the symptoms. So to avoid any unwanted event it is recommended to take your dog to a vet for a proper checkup.

It will take a while for you to reach the vet, meanwhile give the dog ion-site shock treatment. Cover it with your hands, and rub its back to bring its heartbeat to normal. Keep calling its name to ensure that you are there and you will keep the dog safe. It will keep your dog's vital signs normal (unless there is some internal injury). Also position your dog's head slightly lower to ensure proper and adequate supply of oxygen to the brain. This practice can save your dog from slipping into a coma due to shock, if it's fortunate enough to escape massive injuries.

Onsite shock treatment also includes the following:

- Restrain the dog immediately
- Sudden impact instantly disturbs the breathing function in dogs so clear all air passages to ensure adequate supply of oxygen to the dog
- If the dog is bleeding, apply a bandage to stop the bleeding because it can add to the blood loss in case the dog is bleeding internally too
- Look for fractures and sprains and protect external injuries from further damage
- Keep the dog warm to stop loss of body heat and wrap it in some blanket
- Rush to a veterinarian for detailed inspection and proper treatment

What to Avoid in Shock Treatment

Only knowing the things that you should do to treat your dog in shock is not enough, you must also be aware of the practices that you should avoid when giving your dog immediate treatment. Have a look at some of these practices:

- You must not move the dog immediately after the accident, even if it seems fine to you. Internal injuries or bleeding don't have instant impact but movements can quicken the process of blood loss. Plus, an injured dog can't afford to lose calories and energy, so to keep its blood pressure and other vital signs normal and let it rest.
- Applying heating pads to injuries is a common practice that most dog owners follow. Don't do it, as heating pads can burn the skin of the dog. When the heat penetrates dog's

skin, it causes the veins to dilate, thus increasing the blood requirement. This increases the risk of heart failure.

- You might think that giving an injured dog something to eat or drink might help in keeping its energy levels normal. Well, that's not the case. The process of digestion also requires calories and your dog does not have enough energy to waste. Plus, a dog in shock can also aspirate fluids or food into its lungs and this can cause instant failure of the respiratory system.
- Don't give any oral medicine to your dog without getting it examined by a vet. Medicines can cause a reaction and it can worsen the situation.
- Sometimes the dog might seem normal after an accident and it does not show the symptoms of shock or trauma. Don't conclude that the dog is fine if it seems normal physically. Mental traumas can't be diagnosed immediately but it can lead to grave consequences if not treated properly. So make sure you consult a vet to make sure that your pet is fine and does not need any therapy or any other kind of treatment.
- Don't waste time in treating the dog yourself. Even if you have prior experience of handling dogs, you can't treat an injured dog as there are a number of complications and considerations that you must keep in mind while giving medical treatment to your dog and you must consult a professional vet to give the dog the right treatment as soon as possible.
- Last but not least, never leave an injured dog on its own. When a dog is in trauma, it needs your love and care more than ever. If you are there with your dog and ensure it that it is in safe hands and that nothing is going to happen to it, it will make the dog mentally strong. Willpower and strong nerves are really important to recover from mental traumas. If your dog has faith in you, you can always turn him round the corner.

7. Who to Call in Accidental Situations?

No one can anticipate accidents. Finnish Spitz owners should be prepared to handle accidental situations. When a dog meets an accident, many owners panic. The panic makes the situation worst and can cause harm to the dog. The human brain doesn't work properly when it is in an alarming situation. So, the person makes mistakes when it is panicking. Firstly, accept that your dog has met an accident and then take a deep breath. Think clearly and call for help. Who to call?

Animal Rescue Centers in the US

There are several animal rescue centers and organizations working in the US. These centers are available for help 24/7. If your Finnish Spitz meets an accident, call anyone of these centers and get immediate help.

- (877) 277-7938
- 911
- 311
- 916-429-2457
- 202-452-1100
- (508) 853-0030
- (435) 644-2001

Animal Rescue Centers in the UK

Do not waste your time panicking while your dog is suffering from an injury. Call the nearest dog rescue center and get immediate help.

- 01803-812121
- 0844-248-8181
- 01162-336677
- 0300-1234-999
- 020-7922-7954

Chapter 12: Health Concerns

The Finnish Spitz is a healthy and active breed of dog that does not fall to illnesses and diseases. However, there are certain health conditions that this breed of dogs is prone to catching. It is extremely important for Finnish Spitz owners to know about these conditions so that they are able to protect their dogs from them. The most common health concerns for Finnish Spitz are cataracts, autoimmune disease, epilepsy, contracts, pemphigus fallacious, diabetes, hypothyroidism, hip dysplasia, and much more.

1. Diseases and Viruses to Look Out For

Some diseases in Finnish Spitz are genetic. The best way to buy a dog with no health conditions is to check its medical reports with the breeder. Ask to see the puppy's mother and father, which will give you an idea about the pup you are about to purchase. If your breeder doesn't provide you with proper medical details, get the pup checked by a vet. A complete physical check-up will allow you to find out whether the dog is healthy or not.

Some of the most commonly seen health problems and diseases in this breed of dog are given below.

Hip Dysplasia

Hip dysplasia is a hereditary condition in which the thighbone doesn't fix in the hip joint and makes the dog limp. Some dogs feel pain in this condition. Hip dysplasia can grow to become arthritis. That's why, before you buy a Finnish Spitz, make sure you check the pup's parents. If any one of the parents has this condition, the pup will have it too. Many animal societies and vets do not recommend breeding dogs with hip dysplasia. A Finnish Spitz with hip dysplasia has problem in either one rear leg or both.

Hip dysplasia also occurs due to environmental conditions. If the dog slips or falls, if it has been fed on a high-calorie diet, if it has incurred injuries and much more. If you see the signs of discomfort in your dog, make sure to get an X-ray done.

Epilepsy

Epilepsy is a broad term but is usually associated with fits and seizures. Almost 7% of dogs have epilepsy. However, it is not necessarily that, if your dog is getting seizures, it has epilepsy. There can be a variety of factors causing fits and seizures in your Finnish Spitz. Some of the reasons epilepsy occurs are diabetes, hypoglycemia, intoxication, liver disease, hypoxia, tumors, trauma, hydrocephalus, etc.

Epilepsy is often hereditary and occurs the first time when the dog is 6 months to 5 years of age. Epilepsy is not treatable, however, it can be controlled through proper management. Dogs with epilepsy live a healthy life without major discomfort. When the Finnish Spitz is having seizures, call an emergency helpline immediately. The sooner the dog receives treatment, the greater the chances of its recovery.

Progressive Retinal Atrophy

Progressive retinal atrophy is a condition common in older dogs. In this condition, the nerves behind the eyes degenerate, causing vision problems. Some dogs become blind due to this condition.

Diabetes Miletus

When the insulin level in the pancreas rises, a dog will suffer from diabetes. Diabetes is a disease that might occur due to the food that the dog is eating. If your dog eats commercial dog food, there is a high chance that it will have diabetes. Commercial dog food contains glucose and other elements that raise the insulin level in the blood. Diabetes can be controlled with the help of proper medication and care.

Patellar Luxation

Patellar luxation is a condition in which the kneecap is dislocated due to an injury or accident. Patellar luxation is very painful. If the pain is intense and the dog feels uneasy, visit your vet and get it treated. In some cases, patellar luxation is treatable and in others it might require surgery. Patellar luxation doesn't cause a dramatic change in the lifestyle of the dog and is very manageable if you provide proper care to the dog.

Tape Worms

Tapeworms are common in Finnish Spitz and are present in the dog's intestine. These worms are treatable when diagnosed at an early stage. Tapeworms are not always dangerous for your dog, as some of the worms are naturally present in your dog's intestine.

Skin Diseases

Skin diseases are common in dogs, however, their cause is not defined. Skin infections occur when a dog catches skin-eating bacteria. The most common type of skin disease in Finnish Spitz is pyoderma, which causes pus. If your dog is scratching its skin or its skin is irritated, visit a vet, as the vet is likely to conduct a cytology exam in which he/she will take a sample of the affected skin tissue.

Mange Mites

Mange is a skin parasite that can get to your dog's skin from dirt or soil. This parasite eats the skin and is capable of causing various health problems. Get your dog examined by the vet and follow the treatment to get rid of mange mites.

Ringworm

This is another skin infection caused by bacteria. A dog can catch ringworm from other animals, soil, and fungi on blankets, bedding, and brushes. If your dog is showing the signs of ringworm, take it to the vet where the vet will perform a culture of the dog's hair. Another way the ringworm infection is diagnosed is by examining the affected area with a microscope. There are several types of effective treatment options available for ringworm.

Sporotrichosis

Sporotrichosis is an infection that occurs in the skin tissue when a dog is injured or has an open wound. This type of infection usually occurs in Finnish dogs that spend most of their time outdoors. Sporotrichosis is most commonly seen in Finnish Spitz that live in the wild. This infection affects a wound or cut on the skin when in contact with bushes, trees, etc. This skin infection is caused by fungi and can become extremely dangerous if not treated in time. The diagnosis of this infection can be done through cytology and a fungal culture test. If the infection is not severe, it can be treated using a potassium iodide solution. Some vets also prescribe antibiotics for the treatment of Sporotrichosis.

Blastomycosis

Blastomycosis is a fungal infection that affects adult male fighting dogs the most. This infection affects the skin and other organs of the body. This fungal infection is most common in areas like North Alabama, Ohio, Mississippi, Missouri River Valleys, etc. The parts of the body that get most affected by this fungus include the bones, lungs, urinary tract, brain, reproductive tract, and eyes. This infection may also cause skin lesions and inflammation. Blastomycosis can be diagnosed with the help of cytology or histopathology. This infection is curable with the help of anti-fungal drugs. If the infection has affected the brain and lungs severely, there is a high chance that the infection will not be cured.

Fleas

Fleas are the most common type of parasites that dogs catch. Fleas are found in warmer areas and they lay several eggs on the infested place or animal. These eggs do not stick to the hair or fur of the dog and fall off. These eggs then stick to other dogs and animals. The common signs of a flea infestation are itching of the skin, thickening or discoloration of the skin, anemia, hair loss, and other skin infections. A flea infestation can be treated with the help of medication, powder, a flea collar, anti-flea shampoo, etc. To keep your dog away from fleas, you will need to create a flea-free environment for it. Sometimes fleas are removed from the host but they aren't removed from the environment of the infested area, which doesn't solve the problem completely.

Ticks

Ticks are bloodsucking parasites that can cause illness, skin diseases, irritation, and in the worst case, death. Ticks are easily transferred onto other animals and humans. The diseases that are spread by ticks include Rocky Mountain spotted fever, tularemia, babesiosis,

Colorado tick, Lyme disease, and much more. If the dog has caught a massive tick infestation, it will get anemic.

Ticks cause itchiness and inflammation on the skin. This bloodsucking parasite grows in size after feeding on the blood of the host. This tick can easily be identified by anyone. The best way to get rid of ticks on your dog is to get them removed by the vet. The longer you let the tick stick on the skin, the more blood it is going to suck.

Allergic Inhalant Dermatitis or Atopy

When your dog inhales, ingests, or comes in contact with toxic substances, it catches an allergy. The toxic substance might belong to the environment the dog lives in. Allergic Inhalant Dermatitis is also hereditary. The things that cause this allergy include pollens, dust, dust mites, food proteins, human dander, air-borne molds, and much more.

The common signs of Allergic Inhalant Dermatitis include redness and thickness of the skin, hair loss, and itchiness. In many cases, the dog may develop pus in the skin, which causes more itchiness. The ears, feet, face, and armpits are the areas that get most affected with this allergy. Sometimes this allergy is seasonal and sometimes it doesn't go away with the change of season. This allergy can be treated using non-immunotherapy and immunotherapy methods.

Food Allergies

Many dogs catch allergies from certain food items. Food items like dairy products are said to cause the most allergies in dogs. Allergies caused by food can cause itchiness and redness around the ears, feet, face, armpit, and inguinal areas. In some dogs, food allergies can cause stomach problems. Vets use a dietary trial method to diagnose food allergies in dogs. The treatment of allergies caused by food items includes anti-allergy medicines and hypoallergenic dog food. Some vets also suggest homemade food for dogs that have incurred allergies from food items.

Allergic Contact Dermatitis

This type of dermatitis occurs when a dog comes into contact with a harmful substance or toxins. Allergic contact dermatitis usually occurs from dog products like shampoos, sprays, bedding, sheets, medication, and other chemicals.

This type of allergy makes the skin red, inflamed, and irritated. Vets conduct an environmental test to find out the substance that is causing allergies. The vet will suggest an anti-itching cream for the affected area. The substances that caused the allergy should also be removed from the dog's surroundings.

2. Choosing the Right Vet

Not every vet is certified with your country's department. There are several vets in every locality that declare to be professional experts but lack the education in veterinary care.

A vet is a person that is responsible for taking medical care of your dog. That's why it is extremely essential to choose a vet that can take care of your dog in the most efficient and effective way. The key points in choosing a vet for your Finnish Spitz are:

- Talk to friends and family members that have had experience with a vet.
- Take recommendations from the pet store or breeder you bought your dog from.
- Choose a vet that is good with dogs.
- Make sure the vet handles the dogs and animals gently.
- A good vet is an excellent communicator.
- Do not choose a vet that treats animals in a harsh way.
- A good vet will know how to handle the Finnish Spitz.
- Take your dog to the vet that your breeder took it to because the vet will have a complete history of your dog and will know the right way to handle it.
- If you are moving to another neighborhood, make sure you take recommendations from your vet.
- Choose a vet near your home, as it will be helpful in emergency situations.

- Check your state's veterinary medical board website for licensed vets.
- Make sure that the vet you choose accepts your dog's insurance coverage.
- Visit the vet's clinic to observe the environment and other practitioners in the clinic.
- Observe the hygiene of the clinic.
- Make sure you have a look at the workers in the clinic and the way they treat animals.

3. De-Worming the Pet

Intestinal worms are common in dogs. These worms are present in the stool of the dog and enter the dog's body when it licks its fur or body. These worms can cause several health issues in dogs.

Every dog needs to be de-wormed at the age of 2 weeks and then every two weeks until it is 3 months old. Intestinal worms occur due to poor hygiene, which is usually the case with dogs that are bought from careless breeders or pet shops. This is another reason why people should buy dogs from good breeders.

Intestinal worms can cause vomiting, diarrhea, and weakness in the Finnish Spitz. The vet will examine your dog's feces to look for eggs of the worm. This is the most common method used to diagnose whether your dog has intestinal worms or not. The stool needs to be fresh or else the test might come out to be false.

De-worming starts when a pup is just 2 weeks old. At this time, the pup gets vaccinated every two weeks. Adult dogs should be given the vaccination once every year after their fecal examination. If you don't want your Finnish Spitz to have any more intestinal worms, make sure its environment is clean and hygienic.

4. Neutering and Spaying

There are lots of benefits of spaying or neutering your Finnish Spitz. Neutering or spaying before your dog reaches sexual maturity is the best way to avoid hormone-driven behaviors. Dogs that are not neutered become aggressive, start barking, biting, and much more. So, instead of having an un-neutered or un-spayed Finnish Spitz, it is better to have a spayed or neutered one.

When you are buying the Finnish Spitz, make sure you buy a neutered one. The most common problem with un-neutered dogs is that they show bad behavior. The Finnish Spitz is an active dog that can become hard to handle when in heat. The dogs that are in heat often try to escape or fight with neighboring dogs. Overall, un-neutered dogs aren't attractive and that's why you should consider getting them neutered or spayed. Alternatively, you can get them neutered or spayed yourself. Many vets suggest that the best age for neutering a dog is 6 months. However, due to the advancement in technology, many vets prefer to conduct the surgery at 3 weeks. It is easier to conduct a neutering or spaying surgery when the dog is just a pup. Young dogs do not take a lot of time to recover and the surgery doesn't cause a lot of pain either.

Young pups do not have a lot of fat on their body, which makes it easier for the vet to cut through its skin to operate. Early neutering surgeries are less risky. It is suggested that the dog be neutered before its first heat cycle. If you are considering getting your dog neutered or spayed, contact your vet and get the surgery on your pet insurance cover. Usually neutering doesn't cost a lot and can be performed by local vets. It is best to buy the dog from a breeder or center where the dogs are already neutered or spayed, though.

Another huge advantage of getting your dog neutered or spayed is that such dogs have a low risk of getting mammary cancers, ovarian cysts, pyometra, and much more. Thousands of dogs die of such health conditions annually. If you want your Finnish Spitz to live a healthy life, make sure you get it neutered or spayed.

5. Vaccinations and Shots

Keeping a Finnish Spitz dog healthy requires a lot of effort from the owner. The dog will stay perfectly healthy throughout its life without any major health concerns. However, there are certain vaccinations and shots that your dog will need. Many vaccinations for the Finnish Spitz are injected at an early stage of its life.

The Combo Vaccine

This is the type of vaccine that fights a variety of illnesses and conditions in a dog. Your dog should get a combo vaccine at the age of 4 months. This vaccine is extremely effective for the protection against par influenza, hepatitis, distemper, parvovirus, and leptospirosis.

Rabies Boosters

One of the most important vaccines for Finish Spitz is the rabies booster. A rabies injection is a must by law and the dog is given a single dose when it is 3-6 months old. When the dog is grown-up, the vaccine should be given on an annual basis. Some countries suggest that the vaccine be given once every three years.

Canine Distemper

Canine distemper is a viral infection that causes many health problems in dogs. The vaccine of canine distemper should be given to dogs at the age of 3-6 months. At a later stage, the vaccine should be given once every year.

Canine Parvovirus-2

Canine Parvovirus is a vaccine that is a must for every dog, including the Finnish Spitz. This vaccine should first be given at 6-8 weeks of age. The booster vaccine should be given again at one year.

Canine Adenovirus-2

Canine adenovirus is a liver infection in dogs. The vaccine for this infection should be given for the first time at the age of 6-8 weeks. This vaccine schedule should continue every 3-4weeks until the pup is 12 weeks old. Once the pup has grown into an adult, the vaccine will be given once every 1-year or 3 years.

Bordetella Bronchitiseptica

Bordetella Bronchitiseptica is a serious disease in which the dogs cough. It also causes acute tracheobronchitis, which is a harsher version of the cough that is painful too. The first dose of this vaccine is given at the age of 6-8 weeks and the second dose is given at the age of 12 weeks. This vaccine is then given on an annual basis.

Leptospirosis

Leptospirosis is a fever that may cause pain in the muscles, high-fever, bleeding from the lungs and meningitis. This fever is extremely harmful for dogs and may cause death in the worst cases. The first dose of this vaccine should be given to the Finnish Spitz at 12 weeks of age and the second dose at 18 weeks of age. When the pup has grown up, annual boosters of this vaccine are given to the dog.

6. The Vaccination Schedule

Core vaccines

Core vaccines are the ones that every Finnish Spitz should get. These vaccines are essential for a dog's health and need to be given on a schedule. Core vaccines include distemper, canine adenovirus-2, rabies, and canine parvovirus-2.

Non-core vaccines

Non-core vaccines are the ones that are given to a dog depending on its health conditions and other factors such as weight, age, and much more. Non-core vaccines include canine parainfluenza, leptospirosis, coronavirus, and Bordetella bronchiseptica, and Borrelia burgdorfer.

Most of the vaccinations for the Finnish Spitz are given on an annual basis. Below are some vaccinations that your Finnish Spitz requires.

AGE	VACCINATION
5 weeks	Parvovirus
6-9 weeks	Combination Vaccine
12 weeks or older	Rabies
12-15 weeks	Combination Vaccine
Adult Dogs	Boosters

7. Maintaining Medical Reports
It is extremely essential for Finnish Spitz owners to maintain medical reports of their dog. Medical reports help keep your dog safe

and healthy in times of need and emergencies. Medical reports of your dog will help you get it treated the right way.

Medical records play an important role when you are travelling to other countries with your dog. Vets usually look into a dog's medical history before giving it treatment or medication. It is the complete record of a dog that gives out vital health information to the vets.

Maintain your dog's medical history that includes your dog's allergies, its visit to the vets, the vaccines it has had, the diseases it has, the medical condition of the dog, its previous surgeries, medications it has had, and much more. If you have bought the dog from a pet shop or a breeder, ask for its complete medical history, which will not only help you in determining its health but it will also help you in taking care of the dog in a more effective way.

A fully maintained medical history of your Finnish Spitz will allow you to travel with it to different locations. Every state has different rules regarding the Finnish Spitz and most of them ask for the dog's medical history to find out if the dog is healthy and vaccinated. These reports are proof that your pet is absolutely healthy and ready for travelling.

Medical reports also play an important role when you change vets. Often people move to new locations and they need to get in touch with a new vet. If you haven't maintained your dog's medical history, it will be really hard for the new vet to learn all about your dog. It is extremely important for the new vet to learn everything about the dog. Before moving into your new home, make sure you collect all of your dog's medical files from your previous vet. Take your previous vet's number and let your new vet talk to him/her. This way your previous vet will describe your dog's profile to the new vet, which will make it easy for the vet to examine your dog.

The medical report or history of your Finnish Spitz should contain a complete record of the following things:

- Record of its vaccinations since birth.
- Record of its total number of visits to the vet.
- Record of its operations and surgeries.
- Record of its allergies.

- Record of all the medicines it has had in its entire life.
- Record of the health conditions that the dog has.
- Record of the treatment of any illness or disease.
- Record of its stays in the hospital.
- Complete history of its medication and doses.
- Records of any complication during a treatment or a surgery.
- Record of any accidents or injuries.
- Record of the tests conducted on the dog including blood cultures, x-rays, ultrasounds, etc.

8. Regular Check-Ups

Many Finnish Spitz owners do not realize the importance of regular check-ups. Regular check-ups are a way to make sure the dog is fine. This is a preventative approach and provides pet owners with an opportunity to protect their dogs from major illnesses and health conditions.

It is not necessary for your dog to show signs of illness and weakness. Sometimes a pet is suffering internally without prominent symptoms. That's where check-ups come in. A frequent visit to the vet eliminates the chances of your dog getting sick. When you don't visit the vet regularly, minor illnesses become a huge health concern.

Regular check-ups also help you keep your dog groomed. Choose a local vet for your dog and make sure the vet has experience working with Finnish Spitz dogs.

Chapter 13: Caring for Your Spitz

The Finnish Spitz is an active breed that doesn't like to be confined in small rooms. They need tons of physical exercise to stay fit. Apart from exercise, there are many other concerns for this breed of dog. The Finnish Spitz requires a lot of care from their owners. If the guardian of this dog neglects it basic instincts and caring requirements, this dog becomes aggressive and might fall ill.

1. Exercising Requirements

The Finnish Spitz is a breed that is extremely active by nature. There is no way a Finnish Spitz would do well with people that have no time to spend with the dog. These dogs love to run around, walk, swim, and play, so engaging these dogs in physical exercises is the best way to keep them from getting aggressive.

The Finnish Spitz needs a lot of exercise on a daily basis. When you engage in a physical activity with your dog, it will get closer to you. Small running sessions in the garden or backyard will not be enough for your dog. These dogs need intense exercise that includes jogging in the park, hiking, and much more.

General Exercising Tips for the Finnish Spitz

Follow the tips below to provide your Finnish Spitz with proper physical exercise.

- Take your Finnish Spitz with you on walks.
- The Finnish Spitz is an excellent jogging companion.
- Take your Finnish Spitz along for hiking and other adventures.
- Let your dog swim.
- If you don't have enough time, make sure you designate a playtime for your dog so that it doesn't get bored.
- Exercise is a mental stimulant for the dog, so make sure you do not underestimate it.
- You can play fetch with your Finnish Spitz to keep it entertained.
- Always keep your Finnish Spitz on the leash.
- Do not walk behind your dog, as it will become dominating.

- Always walk ahead of your dog and act as the alpha.
- Take your dog with you whenever you go to the park or outdoors for physical activity.

2. Grooming Tips: Make Your Pet Look Gorgeous

The Finnish Spit has a self-cleaning coat, so it doesn't need frequent baths. However, this breed of dog is furry and requires regular combing to get rid of dead hair.

Grooming is an essential part of every pet's health and care. A groomed pet looks more appealing than an untidy pet. There are certain grooming concerns that every Finnish Spitz owner should be aware of. This way the dog will stay neat and tidy. Moreover, it will boost the dog's physical well being.

Brushing

Brushing is the most important grooming required by Finnish Spitz. These dogs have a heavy coat full of hair that protects them in the cold region they originated from. Their hair sheds twice a year, which makes it absolutely essential for them to be brushed on a daily or weekly basis.

Brushing is essential for keeping your dog's hair clean and tangle-free. The dead hair that gather on the coat might fall off everywhere in the house. Dog hair might cause allergies in humans. The Finnish Spitz has two coats: a soft undercoat and a protective outer coat.

Use a combination of a slicker brush, a shedding blade, and a comb to brush your dog's hair. If you neglect the fur for a long time, the fur will become extremely hard to brush as the hair gets tangled and untidy. To keep your dog's coat soft and smooth, make sure you brush it at least once every week. Brushing also helps in spreading the skin's natural oils and is overall a healthy habit.

Bathing

The Finnish Spitz is the dog of the Arctic, which means they generally stay clean. They are double coated but their coat cleans itself. This means that the Finnish Spitz doesn't require frequent

119

baths unless your dog has jumped into the mud or caught dirt on its fur.

Excessive bathing can kill the natural oils of your dog's skin. However, it is not harmful if you bathe your dog once in a while. Bathing your Finnish Spitz will need some training as the dogs are not used to baths. Bathing will keep your dog protected from various illnesses and infections. It is best to bathe your dog once every 3 months. However, this is not a rule of thumb and you can delay the bath according to your preference.

Bathing keeps your dog neat, clean, shiny, and free of dead hair. Your dog also smells good after bathing due to the shampoo. Do not place your dog on a slippery floor for bathing as it may slip or get injured. Always have a rubber mat or a tub to bathe your dog.

Use lukewarm water and gently pour it over your dog with a hose or a cup. Once the dog is completely wet, gently massage the shampoo on its fur. Be careful when bathing your dog and do not let any water enter its eyes, nose, and ears. Once you have applied shampoo throughout its coat, you can rinse it off.

Soak the water from your dog's skin and fur with the help of a soft towel. You can also use a high intensity dryer, which will shake-off dead hair from the fur.

Hair Trimming

The Finnish Spits will need hair trimming on a frequent basis as the dog has a lot of hair. Dog groomers and vets are extremely expensive and will charge a lot of money for simple hair cutting and trimming. That's why it is better to learn it on your own.

You can easily trim or clip your dog's hair if you have the right type of trimmer. Trimming the Finnish Spitz hair on a regular basis is essential to keep it protected from skin infections and flea infestations. Dogs that have thick fur often develop fleas and lice.

There are several hair trimmers available on the market. Choose the one that is appropriate for trimming the desired length. For the trimming purpose, you will first need to make your dog comfortable with the process. Start trimming from the back of the shoulders to the tail and then trim from under the neck and lower body. Do not trim from the areas where there is less fur.

Be careful when trimming the facial hair of your dog as any unusual movement might hurt the dog. Trimming should be done in a separate room where the dog isn't distracted. If your dog has excessive fur around the ears that makes it hard for you to clean them, trim those using scissors or a clipper.

Nails

Many Finnish Spitz owners do not feel comfortable with trimming their dog's nails because they are scared that they will cut too deep. Trimming the nails is a technical process but can be learned with patience and practice.

Do not try to trim your dog's nails if your dog isn't comfortable with you. Nail trimming requires ample attention and your dog needs to be static or else it may get injured. Provide your dog with play toys to keep it busy while you trim its nails.

Positive reinforcement techniques work best when you are carrying out a challenging task like trimming its nails. Start clipping a little portion of your dog's nails instead of cutting too deep. When your dog lets you trim one nail successfully, offer a treat to create a connection between trimming and treats. This is the only way your dog is going to let you trim its nails without moving or getting aggressive.

If you don't want to cut the nail too deep, make sure you start small. The nail is softer from the part that is closer to the dog's skin. Train your dog to stay calm and still while you are trimming its nails.

Eyes and Ears

A dog like the Finnish Spitz has a heavy coat and doesn't require a lot of cleaning around the areas of the eyes and the ears. However, to ensure cleanliness, one must regularly clean their dog's eyes and ears. The area around the eyes may gather a cloudy liquid that can become infectious and make it difficult for the dog to see properly. Similarly, the ears of the dog might gather dirt and wax that can cause infections and problems in hearing.

To keep their eyes and ears clean, check them regularly. If dirt has gathered around or inside them, use a soft cotton ball or a damp cloth to clean the areas of eyes and ears. Never use a Q-tip to clean your dog's ears as it may be cause injuries and hurt its ear canal. You can also use olive oil or natural oils to clean the dog's ears and eyes.

Teeth

Cleaning your dog's teeth is an essential part of its grooming. Many dogs have dental problems that lead to tooth loss and cavity formation. Sometimes the dog's teeth appear fine and owners do not feel the need to brush their teeth. However, cleaning your dog's teeth will help you keep its gums and teeth protected from cavities, bad breath problems, tartar build-up, and tooth loss. These problems occur due to specific diets and sensitive teeth.

Clean your dog's teeth using a dog toothbrush and toothpaste. Brush your dog's teeth once a week to avoid getting them cleaned by the vet that will not only charge a lot but will also need to sedate your dog. Train your Finnish Spitz to stay calm while you brush its teeth. This will be extremely helpful for you as you will be able to keep it clean without going to the vet. When you neglect your dog's teeth, the tartar and cavity build-up can cause bad breath, which is extremely unbearable.

3. Grooming Tools

The tools that you will require to groom your Finnish Spitz are:

- Slicker, steel or pin hairbrush.
- Baby oil.
- Comb.
- Liquid de-tangler.
- Dog trimmer.
- Dog clipper.
- Pair of scissors.
- Shedding blade.
- Blunt scissor.
- Cotton balls.
- Soft cloth.
- Warm water.

- Mineral oil.
- Styptic powder.
- Sharp nail trimmer.
- Dog shampoo.
- Towels.
- Bathing rubber mat.
- Dog toothbrush.
- Dog toothpaste.

4. Grooming Tips

Grooming requires learning the techniques that your dog will be most comfortable with. You cannot start grooming your dog until it is comfortable with you touching its body. It is suggested that you first bond with your dog and then start grooming it on your own.

Below are some effective tips to help you get through the grooming process without any trouble:

- Train your dog to stay calm during its grooming.
- Use treats and toys to encourage good behavior during grooming.
- Never use extremely hot or cold water to bathe your Spitz.
- Never bathe too frequently as it may kill the natural oils on your dog's skin.
- Excessive bathing also makes the skin dry.
- Replace bathing with brushing.
- If your dog doesn't get under your control while you are trimming its nails, get the job done by a vet.
- Do not use a very hot dryer for your dog's fur.
- Use a gentle shampoo to massage your dog's coat.
- Use anti-flea sprays to protect your dog from fleas and lice.
- Do not let any shampoo get in your dog's eyes, ears, nose, and mouth.
- Don't brush the coat of your dog too harshly as it will damage its skin.
- Remove the knots in the fur using a slicker brush.
- Use a slicker brush before bathing your dog.

5. Feeding Concerns: Food That Is Allowed

The Finnish Spitz is an active breed of dogs that hunts in extremely cold temperatures. These dogs are found in Arctic regions and that's why they require proper nutrition to generate body heat on their own. These dogs stay active throughout their lives and need proper food to stay fit. The Finnish Spitz should be fed a balanced diet that is packed with lean proteins.

The Finnish Spitz cannot eat every food that is present in your home. There are certain food items that can potentially harm your dog's health. Therefore, it is extremely important to know the food items that your dog can eat.

Finnish Spits rely on protein sources because they are carnivores. However, there are other food items that can be added to their diets to provide them with proper nutrition. No matter which food you choose to feed your dog, you will need to check its ingredients. Canned and dry food often contain harmful ingredients that may cause health problems in Finnish Spitz.

Feed your Finnish Spitz food that has an appropriate content of protein, carbohydrates, fats, vitamins, and minerals. Meat is the basic requirement of your Finnish Spitz. However, the right type of meat is the one that comes from a verified source. Do not buy food that contains high amounts of glucose or corn syrup. Ingredients like these can harm your dog's health.

6. Foods To Be Avoided

Just like there are foods that your Finnish Spitz can eat, there are foods that can be poisonous to your dog. The foods that you CANNOT feed your Finnish Spitz are given below:

- Chocolate or cocoa.
- Foods containing animal bi-products.
- Foods containing preservative.
- Foods containing artificial colors.
- Grapes
- Raisins
- Xylitol, which is an artificial sweetener.

7. Can The Spitz Be Your Traveling Companion?

Travelling to the store or an outdoor location with your Finnish Spitz is easier than travelling with it to another country. This is where the legalities come in. You cannot just take your pet with you to any country. There are certain rules and regulations that one needs to follow to travel with their pet.

Every country has different requirements when you are bringing a pet with you. Make sure you are aware of these rules or else you and your pet will end up stuck in a bad situation. Below are some tips for travelling to another country with your Finnish Spitz:

- If you live in the US, you can contact the United States Department of Agriculture to get vital information and help on travelling with a pet.
- Before you decide to take your pet along with you to another country, make sure you contact that country's embassy and learn about their rules and regulations for travelling with pets.
- If you are travelling with your Finnish Spitz by air, you will need to fill out a customs declaration card that will mark you as a traveler with a dog.
- Make sure you have a proper travelling carrier and crate for your dog.
- Animals are treated as luggage and they will be handed over to you at the time of arrival when you receive your baggage.
- Some communities do not allow Finnish Spitz to be walked on the roads or parks.
- To get more help of travelling with your pet, please follow the link: www.aphis.usda.gov
- Every airline has different rules and packages for pet travel.
- Make sure that your Finnish Spitz is part of the permitted pets list for international traveling.
- Do not go for the sedation option for your Finnish Spitz.
- Check with your local requirements before travelling with your Finnish Spitz.
- You will need to submit your dog's medical reports to the embassy before traveling to other countries.

Chapter 14: Protecting the Pet

When you have the Finnish Spitz as a pet, you need to take measures to protect it. Protecting a Finnish Spitz means getting it registered with your local animal society. This is the best way you can keep track of your pet in any situation. Often dogs escape or simply get lost. In times like these, the owner and the dog go under massive stress. The impact of this situation can be minimized by getting your dog registered with the local authorities.

Registering a dog gives it a better chance at living a happy and healthy life. The dogs that are lost never reunite with their families. These missing dogs end up in shelters that keep them in unfavorable environments. Many of these shelters put these dogs to sleep due to the increasing population of homeless animals. The only chance that you have to get reunited with your missing pet is by getting it licensed or registered.

1. Licensing

Licensing your Finnish Spitz is extremely important. Licensing is simply getting your dog registered under the state so that the dog has an identity. Unlicensed dogs are those that are homeless and living in shelters. Many states have made it compulsory for every dog to be licensed after its birth. This is a way for the animal associations to get the exact count of animals. There are several advantages of getting your dog licensed.

Why get a License for your Finnish Spitz?

- Licensed dogs have a better chance at getting reunited with their owners.
- Licensed pets are the ones that have had their vaccinations and rabies shots.
- A license is a proof of your dog's health.
- Getting your dog licensed shows that you are a responsible owner.
- Licensed dogs have a greater chance at living a happy life with their owners.
- Licensed dogs can travel to different locations.
- Licensed dogs are allowed outdoors.

- Licensed dogs if lost will be kept in shelters and pet houses until their owners have been reached.
- Licensed dogs aren't put to sleep.

It is extremely important for every Finnish Spitz owner to get their dog licensed. If you are caught without a license for your dog, you will be charged a hefty amount, which is usually $250 or more. The fee of licensing your dog is far less than the penalty you pay for an unlicensed dog.

How to get a License for your Finnish Spitz?

Getting a license for your Finnish Spitz is not a hard task. There are licensing offices in various states and communities. You can also visit websites of your local license provider on the Internet. Such websites allow licensing through e-mail, which is a more convenient process for many dog owners. Your dog license will need to be updated every year with a little fee.

The Requirements for Licensing

There are certain requirements that every dog owner should know before getting their Finnish Spitz licensed.

- Your Finnish Spitz should be 4 months or older.
- To get your dog licensed, you will need to provide your dog's medical history.
- You will also need to show the vaccinations that your dog has had.
- If you have moved to another state or location, you will need to relicense your dog with that state's licensing department.

2. Pet Insurance

If you are wondering whether to buy a pet insurance plan for your Finnish Spitz or not, it is best to go with the former.

Pet Insurance Is Important

Getting your pet registered and putting a collar around its neck with an ID tag is not enough for its security. You must also get it insured.

This is really important to ensure your dog's safety from accidents and mishaps.

Pet insurance helps you save a lot of money. There are times when you can't afford medical bills or cannot pay for an extremely expensive treatment. These are the times when you need insurance for your dog the most. When you are dealing with the stress of your dog's illness, you cannot handle the stress of collecting a huge sum of money. There are several types of dog insurance that not only offer medical support but the expenses that come along with it.

3. Types of Dog Insurance

There are two major categories of pet insurance: Lifetime and Time Limited.

Lifetime Pet Insurance

Lifetime pet insurance doesn't have a time limit to it, which means that this type of insurance will be more costly than any other type.

Lifetime insurance covers long-term illness, hereditary diseases, pregnancy bills, burial bills, vet bills and much more. This also includes the diseases that the Finnish Spitz is prone to catching. When you go out to buy this type of insurance, make sure you have had your dog checked. Pet insurance is an absolute must these days and will help save a lot of money.

Time Limited Pet Insurance

If your dog meets an accident or an injury, a time limited pet insurance is the one for you. This type of insurance allows you to cover the expenses of the injury, medical bills, and surgery. The time limit for this type of insurance is 12 months. This means that after every 12 months you will need to pay the bill and renew your dog's insurance for another year.

Accident Cover

This type of insurance covers only the medical bills and treatment in case of accidents. If your dog has an accident, this insurance will pay for your dog's treatment or surgery. Some banks have a limit for this cover and if your dog's treatment exceeds that, you will have to pay extra. Long-term illnesses and diseases are not included in this type of cover.

Per Condition with a Time Limit

If your Finnish Spitz has incurred an illness or a disease, Per Condition with a time limit will cover all its vet bills. This cover is very beneficial and affordable for Finnish Spitz owners as it covers every type of bill that is connected to that particular illness. This cover lasts for 12 months and can be renewed after expiry. Whatever bills and treatments you will get for your dog in less than 12 months, it will be covered by this insurance.

Per Condition without Time Limit

This type of pet insurance covers the costs of long-term illnesses and diseases. The cover lasts for 12 months but at the beginning the bank asks for a fixed fee that is higher than that of other types of insurance. However, this cover doesn't pay for re-occurring illnesses. The insurance needs to be renewed every 12 months to keep your dog covered.

Compare Insurance Before You Buy

It is extremely important for pet owners to compare different covers, as some might be better than others. Many banks offer great benefits but ask for a lot of money. Before buying a pet insurance, calculate the benefits you are going to get out of it and the one that suits you the best.

4. The Benefits of Getting Your Dog Insured

There are several benefits of getting your pet insured. Millions of people around the world are spending a lot of money on their pet's care, grooming, and health. With so much demand in the market, pet insurance has become an appealing option for pet owners. If you cannot afford to meet your dog's medical or vet expenses, you might as well buy insurance.

There are several benefits of getting a pet insurance. The list below will convince you to buy insurance for your dog:

- Pet insurance allows you to keep your pet healthy at all times.

- Pet insurance will help you get your dog treated in case of emergencies, accidents, and injuries.

- Pet insurance will help you cover your dog's veterinary bills.

- Pet insurance will cover huge and small expenses of your pet.

- Pet insurance will cost you little and provide you with great benefits.

- Pet insurance will cover your pet's treatment for as long as a year.

- Pet insurance is a guarantee for your dog to live a healthy life.

- Pet insurance will save you from stress.

- Pet insurance will provide cover for your dog's life-long illness.

- Pet insurance helps your dog get immediate treatment in case of accidents and emergencies.

5. Different Pet Insurance Providers

When you don't have enough experience dealing with pets, it becomes extremely challenging to differentiate between different covers. It is always best to ask for suggestions from people that have had experience with dog insurance. You can also look up for different insurance providers on the Internet and choose the one that fits you.

Make sure to compare different companies. Also, be aware that your payments are likely to increase every year as your dog gets older.

6. Poison Control

There are certain emergencies that dog owners need to face with patience. When your Finnish Spitz is poisoned or has ingested a toxic substance, do not lose control. Many dog owners panic when their dogs are intoxicated. They over-react and as a result their dog has to suffer. If your dog has ingested a poisonous substance, call your vet or an animal rescue center.

The next thing you need to do is to collect the toxic substance in a bag. This is really important for the vet or the toxicologist, who will need to examine the substance and the effects it could have on your dog. If the dog has ingested a toxic product from a container, make sure to take the container with you.

Often the dog will not show any signs of toxicity but if you suspect anything, make sure you take your dog immediately to the vet. Sometimes toxic substances take several hours or days to show any signs of reaction. It is better to adopt a preventative approach by dog-proofing your home.

Calling the Rescue Center

The first thing you need to do is to call an animal poison center to get help. Animal rescue and poison centers usually charge a fee for consultation, which is about $65. There are certain questions that they ask the owners to get a better understanding of the situation or the toxicity.

- The breed of your dog.
- Its age.
- Its weight.
- Its sex.
- The symptoms that your dog is showing.
- The toxic substance that the dog came in contact with.
- The amount of toxic substance or agent involved in the accident.
- The name of the toxic substance.
- The exact time of the exposure.

In situations where the dog is having seizures or is unconscious after the exposure, call the poison control center and immediately take your dog to the vet.

Precautionary Measures – The Emergency First-Aid Kit

Emergency situations can occur at anytime. The thing that matters the most is how well you are prepared to deal with it. Your dog's life can be saved if you stay prepared ahead of time. The basic thing is to have an emergency first-aid kit. This kit should contain the following things:

- Saline eye solution.
- A bottle of hydrogen peroxide.
- A syringe.
- Bandage.
- Artificial tear gel.
- A dog carrier.
- Small thermometer.
- Stethoscope.
- Mild grease cutting dishwashing liquid.
- Your dog's favorite food.
- Forceps.

Learn to use the tools in your first-aid kit. A first-aid kit is the only guarantee of the safety of your dog in times of need. With the help of an emergency first-aid kit, you will be able to minimize the impact of poisonous substances. Remember, the kit alone cannot help in toxic and poisonous encounters. Make sure you call the poison center or visit your vet immediately.

To keep your Finnish Spitz protected from toxic substances, you need to know the substances that could harm your dog's health. This is the only way you could keep your dog away from incidents like these. Keep toxic substances out of your dog's reach. Products like detergents, lotions, shampoos, deodorants, pesticides, etc. should be kept in locked cabinets at a height the dog can't reach.

Toxic substances also include the food items that are harmful for your Finnish Spitz health. Keep your home clean and do not let the dog enter the kitchen or peek into the garbage. However, no matter what measures you take, there is no guarantee that your dog will not come across emergencies like these.

Common Symptoms of Poisoning

If your Finnish Spitz has ingested a toxic substance, observe your pet closely. Dogs that are exposed to toxic substances will show signs that will identify that they are under the effect of poison. Below are some symptoms that dogs show when they are exposed to poisonous substances:

- High temperature.
- Breathing is abnormal.
- Under shock.
- Seizures.
- Heart rate is too fast or too slow.
- Discoloration in its mucous membranes.
- Vomiting.
- Coughing blood.
- Pale gums.
- Signs of weakness.

If you notice any of the symptoms mentioned above, contact a vet immediately.

Chapter 15: Common Mistakes to Avoid

Every pet owner makes mistakes and it is absolutely normal to do so. However, there are certain things that can be learned and avoided when you have a pet like the Finnish Spitz. These dogs are generally easy to bring up and only become a problem when the owner fails to treat it the right way. To bond with your Finnish Spitz, you will need to be a loving pet person and extremely affectionate. These dogs love their owner's attention and will become destructive if left alone.

Below are some common mistakes that Finnish Spitz owners make. If you avoid these mistakes, your Finnish Spitz will become your forever companion.

Letting it Become The Alpha

The most important thing to remember when you have the Finnish Spitz as a pet is to have control over it. The Finnish Spitz might become dominant if you let it take control of the house and yourself. These dogs live in the wild and they have a fierce personality. The stronger dogs take over the position of an alpha and rule other dogs in the pack. That's why it is important that the owners of these dogs become the authority. Give commands to your dog and set house rules. Train the dog to follow your rules with a positive approach. This is the only way you can keep your dog sane and well behaved.

Letting It Chew Everything

The biggest mistake that owners make is letting their Finnish Spitz pup chew on their socks, feet, couches, furniture, and much more. This soon becomes a problem when they find their home all messed up.

It is important to maintain discipline and correct your dog when it does something that could become a bad habit in the future. As a pup, these dogs are extremely adorable fur balls and when they chew on things, no one wants to scold them. Do not let your Finnish Spitz pup chew or else it will adopt it as a habit. Use a polite tone to tell your dog to stop chewing.

Another way of putting a stop chewing is to provide your dog with enough chewing toys. Pups that chew are in their teething phase and feel pain and irritation in their gums. That is the reason they take comfort by chewing furniture or shoes. However, when you provide chewing toys to your dog, it is less likely to ruin your furniture and other household items.

Another reason for Finnish Spitz to chew is boredom. The Finnish Spitz is a breed of dogs that doesn't take separation or boredom too well. They usually become destructive when they are left alone. When you will take care of these things, your dog is less likely to develop such habits.

Don't Cut Back On Rewards

When you are training your Finnish Spitz, you need to have a lot of treats and toys in stock. The Finnish Spitz is a fast learner. However, if you do not reward it for its good behavior, it will not learn anything at all. Dogs require a constant reward system that keeps them interested in the learning process.

Offering treats and toys to a dog means that it is a reward for its good behavior during the training process. When you do not reward or appreciate your dog with treats, your dog will lose interest. It may become upset and aggressive. That's why it is extremely important for Finnish Spitz owners to reward their dogs whenever it learns a new trick or listens to commands. Keep your dog happy during the training process by offering treats and toys.

Walking Your Dog Without A Leash

The Finnish Spitz needs a lot of exercise and outdoor activity. These dogs are known for alerting their owners of birds for hunting purposes. They should not live in a confined space and need lots of walking and running. That's why you will need to take them for walks and jogs in the park. Make sure you do not leave your dog off the leash in outdoor places. The Finnish Spitz is not a violent dog, however, it may get shy or suspicious of strangers.

When the Finnish Spitz feels shy or suspicious, it might snap at strangers and the people around it. To avoid situations like these, one should put its dog on the leash when outdoors.

No matter how well your dog is trained, never leave it off the leash. Your dog is trained in an environment that it is comfortable in.

Leaving it Alone

The Finnish Spitz is not a dog that likes loneliness. This breed of dogs is extremely active, playful, and energetic. If they are left alone in the house, they do not react too well. The Finnish Spitz is an affectionate dog. These dogs love being with their owners and guardians. Hence, they cannot be left alone. If you make the mistake of leaving your Finnish Spitz alone at home, you will find your home turned into a mess. Your dog will also start to howl, bark, and make loud noises, which are a nuisance for everyone.

Do not leave your Finnish Spitz unattended. These dogs belong near their owners and not apart from them. When the Finnish Spitz is left alone or without supervision, they become aggressive and extremely destructive. Once the Finnish Spitz considers you careless, it will not be the same around you.

Inconsistency During Training

Training the Finnish Spitz requires consistency and dedication. A dog's brain doesn't work like a human's. It will learn tricks and techniques when they are repeated several times. Many owners make the mistake of not being consistent in training their dogs and end up confusing them.

Inconsistent orders to the dog will confuse it and will not be able to connect the command to the right action. For example, if you are saying 'No' then do not use 'Stop' the other time. This will create problems in training and the dog will not follow any command at all.

If you don't want to ruin your training process, do not show inconsistency in your orders and commands. Moreover, make sure that the other family members in the house use the same commands with your dog.

Not Training the Dog

It is a foolish thing to not train your Finnish Spitz. Many Finnish Spitz owners buy their pet from breeders and pet stores that have trained the dog in advance. So, these people do not feel the need to train their Finnish Spitz. However, their confusion soon clears out when their dog starts to create problems in the house.

Every dog needs to be trained by their owners. Even if your dog is already trained, make sure you make it learn your house rules. The breeder and the pet shop would've trained the dog for their rules. If your dog was trained for a different environment, how can you expect it to behave in your house?

Some Finnish Spitz dogs do not like to switch places because they are loyal companions. When they are moved into a new family, they do not adapt to it quickly. They might show signs of aggression, destructive behavior, and depression. The best way to bring them back on track is to train them and spend time with them. Do not ever assume that your dog is perfectly trained and doesn't need further learning.

Experimenting with the Dog's Food

The Finnish Spitz doesn't have particular feeding requirements. However, that doesn't mean you can experiment with its food. Many dog owners like to change their dog's food frequently. Sometimes they end up giving their dog poor quality commercial food. The Finnish Spitz requires a diet that is high in protein, vitamins, minerals, carbohydrates, and fat.

Moreover, these dogs cannot eat everything that we humans eat. Feeding them salty leftovers will be bad for their health. Beware of the food items you are feeding your dog. Feed only healthy dog food specifically created for the Finnish Spitz.

Chapter 16: Confined Spaces and the Finnish Spitz

We keep hearing about well-mannered Finnish Spitz turning aggressive and destructive. So, how does this happen? How do these dogs change their behavior? What makes them turn into wild animals?

There are several reasons due to which the Finnish Spitz may become aggressive, destructive and extremely dangerous. The Finnish Spitz is a wild hunting dog and can turn to its nature if not provided with proper care.

The Finnish Spitz is not a dog that can be kept in kennels, small rooms, and apartments. These dogs require a lot of physical exercise. This active breed of dog cannot stay in confined spaces.

1. Depression and Stress

Dogs that are forced to stay in kennels and confined spaces lose their ability to become good household pets. Similarly, the Finnish Spitz is not a dog that should be kept away from the exposure of people. These social dogs will not survive in small rooms or kennels.

The biggest problem that the Finnish Spitz goes through in confinement is separation anxiety. Separation anxiety usually occurs in dogs that are social and extremely affectionate. The Finnish Spitz is a dog that will love its guardian's company and when forced to live in small spaces, these dogs exhibit signs of stress and depression. They will start to bite on things and bark excessively.

Every animal has a unique brain and nature. The Finnish Spitz is not a dog that will do well alone. If you are planning on buying the Finnish Spitz, make sure that you have enough space in your home and backyard for it to exercise and play. The space in a house is also not enough for the Finnish Spitz and will need to be taken outdoors to provide stimulation to its mind and body. If your Finnish Spitz won't get human attention or space to play, it will lose its mind, become aggressive, violent, and much more

2. Behavioral Problems
What happens when you leave your Finnish Spitz alone in a room for hours?

Many Finnish Spitz owners leave their dog alone when they go to work. When they return, they find their home all messed up and their furniture destroyed. How does this happen?

It is indeed a shock for the owners that expected their FS to stay calm and composed throughout the day. These dogs have a violent streak that shows up when they are left in the home to suffer.

Before you keep your dog in confined spaces, think about the damage it could cause to you, your home, and your relationship with it. If you are heading out, put your dog on the leash and take it along. If you live with your family, make sure there is someone giving your dog company.

3. Caring for Your Dog's Requirements
If you live in an apartment or a room, do not buy a Finnish Spitz. These dogs are extremely active and would want to run free if kept in a room. It is not fair for such an energetic dog to be confined in small spaces.

Unless you are ready to handle such a dog, do not buy one. If you live in a small apartment, take your dog for long walks. You can also take your dog to hiking adventures and picnics. Make sure to dedicate 2 – 4 hours of your day to your dog.

Chapter 17: Interesting Facts about the Finnish Spitz

These adorable furry dogs turn out to be great pets. Below are some interesting facts about this breed:

- The Finnish Spitz is also known as 'Finkies'.
- The Finnish Spitz barks and yodels when it wants to notify its owner of something.
- These dogs are hunters by nature and win awards in Finland.
- The Finnish Spitz gets along with children.
- The Finnish Spitz listens to children more than adults.
- The Finnish Spitz loves to swim.
- The Finnish Spitz bumps its head onto its owner for attention.
- The Finnish Spitz likes to spin in circles.
- The Finnish Spitz puppy is born with black fur, which fades away with time.
- The Finnish Spitz love to lick toes.
- The Finnish Spitz is an ancient breed that was used for hunting purposes.
- The Finnish Spitz is the national dog of Finland.
- The Finnish Spitz is known for pointing out birds and animals to hunters.
- This dog belongs to a non-sporting breed of dogs.
- The Finnish Spitz is also used to boost the confidence of players in a game.

Conclusion

The Finnish Spitz is a clever dog that protects its owner and guardians from threats. These intelligent dogs take time to learn tricks and commands. However, with a consistent, patient, and repetitive approach, they can easily be trained to follow house rules, voice and hand signals.

The Finnish Spitz is a social butterfly but won't do too well with strangers. These dogs require socialization in their early stages of life so that they learn to stay calm around unknown people and animals. This breed of dog doesn't cause a lot of trouble and stays in a good mood most of the time. Their friendly and affectionate nature catches everyone's attention. This furry dog sheds a lot of fur but is easy to groom.

The Finnish Spitz needs to be handled with a lot of care and attention or else they can easily become aggressive and ill mannered. This breed is trained to be nice to humans and is extremely sociable. At first, these dogs are reserved but once they gel with their masters they become protective of them. It is a perfect companion for your outdoor adventures, picnics, and much more. These dogs become a part of the family in no time.

This dog is ideal for people that love to hunt birds. They will alert their masters of the birds with the help of their distinct yodeling sound. The relationship that the Finnish Spitz develops with its owners is irreplaceable and an emotional one. These dogs are extremely possessive about their master and will keep them safe at any cost. This exceptional breed of dogs proves to be a complete pet for loving masters.

At first, this dog will be challenging to own and train, but with determination I am sure that this dog will be a great companion and addition to your home. I hope you have learned all you need to know about this dog and its needs and habits.

Thank you for reading this book.

Published by IMB Publishing 2015

52335783R00079

Made in the USA
Lexington, KY
12 September 2019